MW00846806

A PATHWAY TO EXPERIENCE GOD'S PRESENCE

Nine Devotional Messages
to Lead You to God's
Revealed Presence

DR. RICKY BRANHAM

"READINGS FOR YOUR PRAYER CLOSET"
DEVOTIONAL MESSAGE SERIES — BOOK 2

A Pathway to Experience God's Presence

Trilogy Christian Publishers
A Wholly Owned Subsidiary of Trinity Broadcasting Network
2442 Michelle Drive, Tustin, CA 92780

Trilogy Christian Publishing/TBN and colophon are trademarks of Trinity Broadcasting Network.

Photography by: Christie Stevens Photography & Holiday Photography

For information about special discounts for bulk purchases, please contact Trilogy Christian Publishing.

Trilogy Disclaimer: The views and content expressed in this book are those of the author and may not necessarily reflect the views and doctrine of Trilogy Christian Publishing or the Trinity Broadcasting Network.

10 9 8 7 6 5 4 3 2 1
Library of Congress Cataloging-in-Publication Data is available.

ISBN: 978-8-89041-262-1
E-ISBN: 978-8-89041-263-8

DEDICATION

To my beautiful, smart, and adoring wife, Victoria. Your support is immeasurable, and you are a true example of a Proverbs 31 wife and mother.

To our kids, Ricky, Riley, and Vera, for whom I know God has amazing things planned. The joy you have brought to our home is fulfilling. God has revealed His presence to you all many times, and it is just the beginning.

To my grandparents in Heaven, Robert and Lena Branham, who taught me the ways and things of God from a young age.

ACKNOWLEDGMENTS

Thanks to my mother, father, stepfather, and stepmother, who have stood behind my calling from the beginning.

Thanks to my brother, Joshua Branham, for his listening ear, for his editing and graphic designing skills, and for supporting my ministry in every way.

Thanks to Robert Holthouse of Robert Holthouse Pro-ductions, who uses his video production talents to help me spread the Word of God all over the world.

CONTENTS

INTRODUCTION

Do you desire to experience God's presence? God wants to reveal His presence to you so that you can experience all the blessings He has for you. When God makes His presence known, miracles take place. By reading this book, you will be blessed spiritually, physically, mentally, emotionally, relationally, and financially through the presence of the Lord. I will show you through the Word of God how you can regularly experience God's presence and receive His abundant blessings in every area of your life.

God reveals Himself to the person who seeks Him. God revealed to me, while I was seeking Him, a series of biblical steps to experience God's presence regularly. I call these biblical steps a "pathway." I break down this pathway into nine devotional messages, so you, too, can practice His presence regularly and be blessed by Him. Each devotional message in this book contains a central biblical theme, many Bible Scriptures, and a message from God for you. Each devotional message is like a small sermon in written form. These devotional messages can be read anywhere and anytime to help you grow in the Lord. They can also be used to help prepare sermons, Sunday school lessons, and for general Bible discussions. You will find the most value in them when they are read alone in your prayer closet. God will use them to speak to you in a powerful way during your quiet time with Him, and it will change your life forever. Be ready to experience the greatness that is, God's presence.

Why a Book about Experiencing God's Presence?

I have been blessed to be a minister of the Gospel since the age of sixteen. I have always sought to know God in a deeper way. In March 2020, when the COVID-19 pandemic started to hit the world hard, I began diligently, or carefully, seeking God like never before. I did this while alone in my prayer closet, also known as my bedroom. I started seeking God like this because of the immense desire that I had, from the Holy Spirit drawing me, to know Him in a deeper way.

As a result of seeking God, I received many blessings. I started to hear and recognize God's voice clearer than ever, receive new revelations from God's Word, see and feel His power, and develop a deeper relationship, fellowship, and friendship with Him. He became my "exceeding great reward" (Genesis 15:1). During this period of time, while I was alone seeking God, He revealed to me through His leading and His Word a series of biblical steps to experience His presence regularly. I call these biblical steps a "pathway." It is the pathway that God gave to me to share with others. I continue to this day following the pathway God showed me, and God continues to reveal Himself to me, blessing me and others in great ways.

As a television minister, I receive countless prayer requests. My wife and I love to release our faith and agree in prayer for the power of God to answer all the prayer requests received. Glory be to God; He hears all our prayers and loves to answer them. People are saved, healed, delivered, blessed, and have experienced other miracles. It is wonderful and godly to reach out to others for agreement in prayer, and you should do this often (Matthew 18:19). However, there are times when you are in need for something quickly, and you cannot wait for someone else to pray. Maybe you cannot find someone to agree in faith with you right away. Therefore, I want you to understand how to have a revelation of God's presence so you can receive your miracle quickly and on your own. The pathway I will show you will help you to experience God's presence and receive your miracle quickly and on your own.

The final idea for this book came together after I wrote the book *Psalm 23: A Psalm for the Living*, which is the first in my series "Readings for Your Prayer Closet". The primary focus of the first book is the blessings of God that He has for you in this life and in Heaven eternally. I also briefly explained in the beginning of that book: how to experience God's presence; how God oftentimes uses the awareness of His presence to reveal His will; how the Good Shepherd uses the revealing of His will to lead you; and how if you follow His leading and obey, you will be led to receive an abundance of God's blessings. Also in book one, I used a devotional message format, for which God gave me the inspiration, to explain Psalm 23. Each devotional message contained a central biblical theme, many Bible Scriptures, and a message from God for you. Each devotional message was like a small sermon in written form.

This second book in my series "Readings for Your Prayer Closet," *A Pathway to Experience God's Presence*, will expand on many of the things I talked about in the beginning of book one. I will make many references to the Lord as your Shepherd in this book because it is the Spirit of God who leads you to experience God's presence regularly. This book will primarily focus on how to experience God's presence through the revelation of the pathway, or biblical steps, that God showed me, so you can receive your miracle quickly and on your own. You do not have to read book one in order to understand what I am going to show you. The pathway I will show you will be broken down into nine devotional messages. I want each devotional message to enlighten you with an understanding of God's revealed presence, to be biblically based, and to be read, studied, and meditated on, whenever possible, in your quiet time with God. Get ready to experience God and receive all that He has for you!

GOD'S PRESENCE

People are starting to become hungry to experience God's presence in their lives. They want to experience God's presence so they will know His will, feel His power in their lives, and receive His blessings. They need Him to save, heal, deliver, bless, and perform other miracles. All this can happen when His mighty presence is revealed. Many do not understand how the presence of God works and what it means for God's presence to be made visible. This could become a deep theological discussion, but it does not need to be because God's Word makes it simple. First, let me begin by going over a few basic biblical principles that relate to the presence of God.

Three Basic Principles That Relate to the Presence of the Trinity

1) OMNIPRESENT

The Trinity—God the Father, God the Son, and God the Holy Spirit—are omnipresent, which means They are present everywhere. The Bible shows that the Trinity's presence is with you wherever you are, even when you do not think They are there, recognize Them, or realize Them. The Trinity is with you from the womb, while you live life on this earth, and throughout your eternal life.

Whither shall I go from thy spirit? Or whither shall I
flee from thy presence?
If I ascend up into heaven, thou art there: if I make
my bed in hell, behold, thou art there.
If I take the wings of the morning, and dwell in the
uttermost parts of the sea;
Even there shall thy hand lead me, and thy right hand
shall hold me.
If I say, Surely the darkness shall cover me; even the
night shall be light about me.
Yea, the darkness hideth not from thee; but the night
shineth as the day: the darkness and the light are
both alike to thee.
For thou hast possessed my reins: thou hast covered me
in my mother's womb.

— Psalm 139:7–13

The Hebrew word for "presence" in verse 7 of Psalm 139 is *pamim* (6440), which means presence or faces. It is a plural word indicating more than one face, which shows the Trinity. The Trinity may not always be physically present in body, but Their presence is everywhere, and They see everything.

The eyes of the LORD *are in every place, beholding the*
evil and the good.

— Proverbs 15:3

2) LIVES IN THE CHRISTIAN

The Spirit of God lives in the one who repents (changes their mind by turning from all their sins, asks God to forgive them of all their sins, and forgives everyone), confesses (with their mouths by speaking out loud), and accepts Jesus Christ as their Lord (takes Him as their Master, Owner, and Ruler) and personal Savior (One who saves believers from all their sins and gives them a home in Heaven). God's presence, through the Holy Spirit, literally lives inside the Christian.

> *Know ye not that ye are the temple of God, and that the Spirit of God dwelleth in you?*
> — 1 Corinthians 3:16

3) NEVER LEAVES THE CHRISTIAN

God promises to never leave nor forsake the one who remains in Christ. You can turn your back on Him, but He will never turn His back on you. In other words, God's presence, the Holy Spirit, will never be taken from one of His children.

> *Let your conversation be without covetousness; and be content with such things as ye have: for he hath said, I will never leave thee, nor forsake thee.*
> — Hebrews 13:5

Experiencing God's Presence

As I have shown you through the Bible, the presence of God is everywhere. However, you may not be aware of His presence because He has not been making Himself known to you, which is what I mean when I say you are not "experiencing God's presence." In other words, God is not revealing or manifesting Himself to you. The words *manifest*, *manifestation*, and *manifested* are biblical words that mean "to make visible." If

God is not manifesting Himself to you, then He is not making Himself visible to you in a way so that you can experience Him. God is not making Himself known to you.

(*Important to note*: Unfortunately, the devil has been using false religions, New Age garbage, and other occult belief systems by having them adopt and use biblical words to try to make them their own by twisting the meaning the Bible originally intended. This has confused a lot of Christians because now when they hear certain words, they think they are ungodly words when they originally came from the Bible. For example, words like *manifest*, *manifestation*, and *manifested* are biblical words that simply mean "to make visible." Also, biblical words like *meditate* and *meditation* simply mean "to ponder" or "to think on." The devil is a thief that takes godly things and twists them, putting them in false religions. Therefore, when I use these biblical words, you can be assured that I use them in a biblical way only. I am a Christian who completely sticks to the Word of God. I only follow what is found in the Bible — from Genesis all the way through Revelation. Furthermore, you should never add to the Word of God or take away from the Word of God (Revelation 22:18–19).)

If God is choosing not to reveal Himself to you, there could be several reasons. It could be because there is sin in your life, or it is not His perfect timing, or you simply lack biblical knowledge on what to do in order to have God reveal Himself to you. If you are a committed follower of Jesus and you are doing your best to live for Him, God will show Himself to you in due season. The pathway I will show you in this book will teach you biblical principles that will get you ready for God to reveal Himself. I have found that by following these biblical principles, I regularly experience seasons of God's presence, and you will also.

> *To every thing there is a season, and a time to every purpose under the heaven.*
>
> — Ecclesiastes 3:1

Until God's presence manifests to you, you should live by faith knowing He is always there, even when He is not presenting Himself to you.

> *For therein is the righteousness of God revealed from faith to faith: as it is written, The just shall live by faith.*
>
> — Romans 1:17

God has special reasons for wanting to reveal Himself to you. Oftentimes, it is so you can know His will, be blessed, and bless others. This is why it is important that you are doing the right things for this to happen. Then, when God sees you are ready, He will choose to make Himself known to you. This is what I mean when I say "experiencing God's presence." Here are some terms I use that also mean the same thing as experiencing God's presence: God's presence arriving; finding God's presence; God becoming real to you; being taken into God's presence; practicing God's presence; God showing up; God coming to you; God manifesting Himself to you; God revealing Himself to you, or anything similar. Summed up even simpler: you are experiencing God's presence. Also, know that the complete Trinity is always present when you are experiencing God's presence, as I will discuss this in more detail in devotional message two. The biblical steps to experience God's presence frequently is what I refer to as a pathway.

How God Reveals His Presence

God can reveal His presence to you in a limitless number of ways. I will share with you some of the ways that I have experienced God's presence, combined with ways the Bible describes. Remember, this is not a complete list because there are a host of ways that God may reveal His presence to you. God may reveal His presence to you by pressing something on your heart and mind by giving you a promise, godly thought, idea, or answer to a problem or situation. He may make the Word of God come alive so that it really speaks to you when you are reading it, studying it, or meditating on it. You may hear an audible voice, have a vision, or have a godly dream. He may heal your body or give your body rest. He may answer one or several of your prayers. He may send someone to speak a word from God to you. He may open or close a door of opportunity. The presence of God may cause you to experience the fruit of the Spirit, be still, be in awe of Him, be silent, or even cry. He may manifest His presence to you by causing you to physically feel or see a display of His power.

The number-one way God has manifested His presence to me during my alone times with Him is by pressing something on my heart and mind through His still, small voice, which many times leaves me in awe of Him. This pressing has happened to me oftentimes in the form of a promise, godly thought, idea, or answer to a problem or situation. When this pressing happens, I know beyond a shadow of a doubt that it is God speaking to me. I do not have to question or wonder because I know His voice. I know His voice because I have spent time with Him, I have a relationship with Him, and He makes His voice clear. This is what Jesus taught when He said His sheep know His voice.

> *To him the porter openeth; and the sheep hear his voice: and he calleth his own sheep by name, and leadeth them out.*
> *And when he putteth forth his own sheep, he goeth before them, and the sheep follow him: for they know his voice.*
> *And a stranger will they not follow, but will flee from him: for they know not the voice of strangers.*
>   — John 10:3–5

> *My sheep hear my voice, and I know them, and they follow me.*
>   — John 10:27

In whatever way God decides to tell you He is there by becoming real to you, by manifesting His presence to you, you will know it. Anytime God reveals Himself to you, it will always be in agreement with God's Holy Word, the Bible.

Experiencing God's Presence Produces Blessings

If you know that God is with you always, why do you need Him to reveal Himself to you? There is always an important reason God wants you to know His presence is there. He may reveal His presence to you for a host of reasons. Oftentimes, it is so you can know His will and so He can lead you and others to His prepared blessings. Your walk with God will change when you discover He has a perfect plan for your life that includes prepared blessings.

> *For I know the thoughts that I think toward you, saith the LORD, thoughts of peace, and not of evil, to give you an expected end.*
>
> — Jeremiah 29:11

You have a purpose. There is a plan for you. You do not have to wander aimlessly in this life, trying to figure out what to do. You have the Good Shepherd beside you, who is leading you along righteous paths (Psalm 23:3). He has planned these paths for you because He wants to bless you. The blessings of God in your life are not an accident; they have been prepared (Psalm 23:5). All you have to do is follow and obey Him. Then you will experience all the great things He has prepared for you, and God will be glorified. You will reap blessings in every area of your life on this earth and in eternal life with Him (Psalm 23:1–6).

There are many Scriptures that show God's will is to bless you with His overflow/riches. Here are several for you to study: Genesis 1–2; Exodus 34:6; 1 Chronicles 4:10; 1 Chronicles 29:11–12; Nehemiah 1:11; Job 36:11; Psalm 84:11; Psalm 112:1–3; Proverbs 8:21; Proverbs 11:24; Proverbs 13:22; Proverbs 14:11; Proverbs 15:6; Proverbs 22:4; Proverbs 28:20; Ecclesiastes 5:19; Isaiah 1:19; Matthew 7:7; Mark 10:29–30; Mark 11:22–24; John 10:10; Galatians 3:29; 1 Timothy 6:17–19; 3 John 2. If you want more details on the blessings of God, my book *Psalm 23: A Psalm for the Living* will teach you about the blessings of God that He has for you in this life and in Heaven eternally. God is no respecter of persons, meaning that what He has done for one person, He will do for another.

> *For there is no respect of persons with God.*
> — Romans 2:11

So, it is clear that God plans to bless you and others, and experiencing His presence will cause this to happen. Let me break down even more clearly for you the way this process frequently works: First, God has prepared blessings. He reveals His presence to you. He uses His presence to reveal His will. The Good Shepherd uses the revealing of His will to lead you. Finally, if you follow and obey His leading, a great blessing or miracle will take place that will glorify God. Remember, the Bible is clear that God wants to bless you and bless others so that He can be glorified.

> *The thief cometh not, but for to steal, and to kill, and to destroy: I am come that they might have life, and that they might have it more abundantly.*
> — John 10:10

> *Even every one that is called by my name: for I have created him for my glory, I have formed him; yea, I have made him.*
> — Isaiah 43:7

But as truly as I live, all the earth shall be filled with the glory of the LORD.

— Numbers 14:21

Now let me break down even further the way this process frequently works, using an example. First, as we have seen, God has a plan to bless you and others. He makes Himself known to you by pressing on your heart and mind something He wants you to do. For this example, let's imagine He is telling you that His will is for you to witness to a particular family member about the love and forgiveness of Jesus Christ. Therefore, you know He is leading you to do this, and you are following His leading. The next time you see that family member, God brings about the perfect timing for you to witness to that person, and you are obedient to the Lord's request. The family member repents, confesses, and accepts Jesus Christ as their Lord and personal Savior. You are tremendously blessed to be used by God to win someone for Him, and you feel especially blessed that it is a family member. Furthermore, this newly saved, born-again Christian is now also blessed because he/she will live eternally in Heaven instead of Hell. Everything that has taken place perfectly matches the Word of God, and God is glorified.

God had prepared blessings for me and millions of people around the world using television, radio, and social media. It all began in March 2020, when I started diligently seeking God's face and His ways like never before while alone in my prayer closet, also known as my bedroom. Diligently seeking God means to well and thoroughly desire to know Him and His ways by spending time with Him. As a result, I started experiencing the presence of God regularly. During one of these times in my prayer closet, God pressed on my heart and mind to begin a Facebook ministry because many churches were closed due to the COVID-19 pandemic. I was rather reluctant to begin this type of ministry, but I followed His leading and obeyed.

On September 30, 2020, I met with a preacher who was on television who had seen my Facebook sermons. He told me he liked how biblically based they were. The preacher asked me if I had ever thought about television ministry. He did not know that when I was sixteen and first started preaching, I wanted to be a television minister. When he asked me that question, something came alive in me and stirred again my desire to preach on television. However, I did not know how I could preach on television, considering I lived in a small community and pastored a small church. I went to the Lord and prayed about it in my prayer closet. I experienced the presence of the Lord, and He pressed on my heart and mind what to do next.

The Lord led me to the next step of contacting WGGN-TV 52, which I did. On October 21, 2020, exactly three weeks from when I was asked if I had ever thought about television ministry, I had a television contract with WGGN-TV 52 and was taping in their studio. My television program, *Ricky Branham Ministries*, first aired on November 25, 2020, at 6 p.m., on WGGN-TV 52 in Ohio. The title of my first television sermon was "Remember Your Testimonies." My first radio program aired on WLRD 96.9 FM in Ohio on November 29, 2020. On February 2, 2021, my television program aired for the first time on WLLA-TV 64 in Michigan. On June 5, 2021, my television program first aired nationally through the GEB Television Network, which is owned and operated by Oral Roberts University.

My television program has since expanded to many more networks in the United States, and it continues to grow nationally and internationally. It airs in all fifty states and reaches a potential audience of over seventy-eight million people a week and growing. Search on your television for your local TV listing: *Ricky Branham Ministries*. God has amazed me with how He has wonderfully orchestrated everything regarding this television ministry. He has given me a great Christian agent, the perfect church for production, an amazingly talented producer, a quality closed-captioning company to work with, and the list goes on. The television networks have been an absolute pleasure to work with as we work together to spread God's Word. All this has been wonderfully orchestrated by God for this small-town preacher. God has done it in such a way that only He can receive the glory. God's blessings have literally chased me down!

I regularly seek the Lord to know His will in the areas of television, radio, and social media. He continues to reveal Himself to me to show me His will. I follow and obey His leading. As a result, I have experienced great blessings and many miracles, and so have others. I have been blessed to see many people around the world repent, confess, and accept Jesus Christ as their Lord and personal Savior. God is being glorified all over the world. My prayer is that I would see one million people come to know Jesus Christ as their Lord and personal Savior from the ministry He has gifted me with.

A PATHWAY TO EXPERIENCE GOD'S PRESENCE

God has revealed His presence to me on a variety of occasions and various situations inside the church. The result of His revealed presence to me inside the church is that He has spoken to me many times and in many ways, and I have felt and seen the power of God. I was called to preach at the age of sixteen during a church service. I will share more about that toward the end of this book. Inside the church, I have been healed, I have seen others healed, and I have felt and seen His power while worshiping and praying. I have witnessed many mighty miracles take place inside the church.

God revealed His presence to me when I visited the Asbury College Revival. I had been hearing a lot about the revival at Asbury, which began on February 8, 2023. I had been wondering if it was the real deal or not when I received an unexpected phone call on the morning of February 17, 2023, from Rev. Johnny Hagar, who lives in Kentucky. Rev. Hagar had called just to talk when he casually mentioned that he had been to the Asbury College Revival. I asked him if it was the real deal, and he said it was. I began to think that maybe I should go there and seek the Lord about two important areas in which I needed God to move. Of course, I knew that God could answer my prayers anywhere, but I eventually had an inner sense of direction and a peace from God that I should go there and seek Him for my answers.

On February 19, 2023, my son, Ricky, and I made the trip to Hughes Auditorium at Asbury College to experience the revival for ourselves. As we got closer to the college, we noticed a big electronic sign saying that it was over capacity and there would be no further entry. Nevertheless, we pressed on. We finally made it to campus, only to find a line to get into the revival that was about a half-mile long. You could only go in the main building after someone came out because it was filled to capacity. As we were walking along the line, we met a mother named Courtney who had her three kids with her. God used her in a mighty way. She allowed us to get in line with her family, and a little over two hours later, we were in the main revival location. God worked everything out as He always does.

Once we were inside, God immediately revealed His presence to me as I felt His power in such a mighty way. My thirteen-year-old son, Ricky, raised his hands in worship on his own. I have never seen him do that before, so I knew he was feeling the power of God. God also made Himself known to me by speaking to me to just worship Him, listen to the message, and not pray about my two needs for at least an hour. God was leading me, and I obeyed. A little after an hour, I started praying about my two big requests, and God answered my prayers by giving me two great promises. I knew in faith that they were answered. I am not saying every aspect of the Asbury College Revival was perfect, but I am saying that I saw many people come to know Jesus Christ as their Lord and personal Savior in that place, and He was glorified. Furthermore, I experienced the revealed presence of God while there, and He answered the two big prayer requests that I had made of Him.

God has revealed His presence to me on a variety of occasions and various situations outside the church as well. The result of His revealed presence to me outside the church is that He has spoken to me many times and in many ways, and I have felt and seen the power of God. Outside the church, I have been healed, I have seen others healed, and I have felt and seen His power while worshiping and praying. I have witnessed many mighty miracles take place outside the church.

I have experienced the presence of God the most when I have been by myself diligently seeking Him. It has been during these alone times that He has revealed to me many of His most important promises, revelations, and secrets by speaking to me in many ways, including through the Word of God. This is when God revealed to me through His leading and His Word a series of biblical steps, a pathway, to experience His presence regularly. The pathway I will show you is a great way to seek the Lord. Think of the pathway as a process of going deeper in the Lord and His Kingdom as you diligently seek Him first. God promises to reward, or bless, the one who diligently seeks after Him first. He has blessed me in so many ways that I cannot count them all, and He will do the same for you.

> *But without faith it is impossible to please him: for he that cometh to God must believe that he is, and that he is a rewarder of them that diligently seek him.*
> — Hebrews 11:6

God wants to bless you, and there is nothing wrong with receiving the blessings of God. However, remember, it is clear you are to seek the Kingdom of God first, which means the sovereignty of God over everything. In simpler terms, seek God and His will first. Seek after Him, not things, and He will bless you.

> *But seek ye first the kingdom of God, and his righ-*
> *teousness; and all these things shall be added unto you.*
> — Matthew 6:33

Notice I said earlier there is "a" pathway to experience God's presence — this is not the only pathway. God can reveal His presence to you anywhere, at any time, and with anyone else around. However, any pathway God uses to take you into His revealed presence always begins with Jesus Christ. There are no exceptions to this rule. In other words, everything starts with Jesus.

> *Jesus saith unto him, I am the way, the truth, and the*
> *life: no man cometh unto the Father, but by me.*
> — John 14:6

Nine Biblical Steps on the Pathway

The powerful pathway that God has shown me, which you take to experience His presence regularly, has always worked for me. I know it will work for you. Furthermore, it is the primary way that I seek God, and you can use the pathway as a way to seek the Lord yourself. Here are the nine biblical steps I will share with you through the upcoming devotional messages:

1. Salvation
2. Alone with God
3. Pray
4. Thanksgiving
5. Praise
6. Worship
7. Read the Bible
8. Meditate on the Bible
9. Wait on God

How to Use the Pathway

It is essential to let God lead you in every biblical step of the pathway, because these are spiritual biblical steps filled with glorious spiritual experiences. The biblical steps will draw you closer to God as you use them to seek Him. The biblical steps are not difficult, and they are not meant to be. Therefore, my primary focus in each biblical step will be on the importance of that biblical step, rather than on how to accomplish that biblical step in-depth. If something in-depth is required, I know the Holy Spirit will help you. Keep progressing through the biblical steps until God reveals His presence to you and He will in due season. Once you experience God's presence, let Him lead you as to whether you continue with the remaining biblical steps. If you are unsure whether to continue once God has revealed Himself to you, I recommend you continue because He may reveal Himself to you in a new, different, or deeper way in another biblical step. You may experience Him in one, two, or several of the biblical steps. He may lead you to go back and repeat one or several of the biblical steps. Or, once

His presence is revealed to you, it may just leave you speechless and in awe of Him. Let the Holy Spirit lead you.

After you have read all the devotional messages, you are ready to practice these biblical steps regularly as a way to seek the Lord. You may be wondering how much time you should set apart to go through these biblical steps. Obviously, there are many variables to this answer. However, I recommend starting with thirty minutes a day and adjusting from there as God leads you. For some of you, making the time for the pathway will be the hardest part of the pathway. I typically spend at least one hour at a time, every day, going through these biblical steps. Sometimes I will even go through this process more than once a day. When I have a day that I do not spend time with God going through the pathway, I really miss it. Spending time with God is not a chore, and it is not burdensome. It is a peaceful, loving, and blessed experience.

Now Is the Time!

God will be calling His children to that meeting place in the sky soon, the event known as the Rapture, because we are living in the last days. Are you ready?

> *Then we which are alive and remain shall be caught*
> *up together with them in the clouds, to meet the Lord*
> *in the air: and so shall we ever be with the Lord.*
> — 1 Thessalonians 4:17

Because God could be calling you home at any time, now is the time to experience the presence of God. Now is the time to receive all that He has for you. God promised that He would pour out His Spirit on all flesh in the last days.

And it shall come to pass in the last days, saith God, I will pour out of my Spirit upon all flesh: and your sons and your daughters shall prophesy, and your young men shall see visions, and your old men shall dream dreams.

— Acts 2:17

Just as I have experienced God's presence and my life has changed in every way for the better, you, too, should get ready for the same to happen to you. Now is the time!

NINE DEVOTIONAL MESSAGES ON THE PATHWAY

1. Salvation

2. Alone with God

3. Pray

4. Thanksgiving

5. Praise

6. Worship

7. Read the Bible

8. Meditate on the Bible

9. Wait on God

DEVOTIONAL 1

Salvation

For God so loved the world, that he gave his only begotten Son, that whosoever believeth in him should not perish, but have everlasting life.

— John 3:16

Do you desire for you and your family to have a better life spiritually, physically, mentally, emotionally, relationally, and financially? I know you do because God has led you to this book for a reason. All these blessings can be found by experiencing God's presence regularly, and I will show you how. Jesus Christ is the key that unlocks the blessings of God in this life and in Heaven eternally through salvation in Him. I became saved when I was fifteen years old. From that point on, I truly became serious about serving God with everything I had. I have never regretted that decision, and I have never met anyone who has regretted serving Jesus. However, I have met people who wished they had started serving God sooner. Now it is time to learn that the Shepherd leads you, His sheep, to spiritual rest through salvation, which is the first and most important biblical step on the pathway to experiencing the presence of God regularly.

Salvation takes into account all the redemptive acts and processes of God the Father, God the Son, and God the Holy

Spirit. Salvation begins on earth and will culminate in Heaven with the greatest blessing ever: dwelling with God forever. The reason that salvation is the first and most important biblical step on the pathway is because that is the most important thing to the Trinity. God wants a personal relationship with you, and He wants you to go to Heaven more than anything else. Salvation must first take place if you want to grow in the Lord. Salvation is the starting point on the pathway to having God reveal Himself to you. Salvation begins when you repent (change your mind by turning from all your sins, ask God to forgive you of all your sins, and forgive everyone), confess (with your mouth by speaking out loud), and accept Jesus Christ as your Lord (take Him as your Master, Owner, and Ruler) and personal Savior (One who saves believers from all their sins and gives them a home in Heaven). The Holy Spirit draws you and helps you in choosing to pray the Prayer of Salvation. I will lead you in the Prayer of Salvation later in this devotional message, so get ready to pray. The moment of your salvation starts your personal relationship with God the Father, God the Son, and God the Holy Spirit.

I love the fact that God desires a relationship with everyone in the entire world. The fact that God gave His Son, Jesus, so that you could go to Heaven proves His love and desire to have a relationship with you (John 3:16). He desires to be your Heavenly Father. To think that the God of all creation wants to have a relationship, fellowship, and friendship with you is amazing. He wants to be your Good Shepherd, the One who leads you through salvation to an overflow of His blessings on earth, and finally into eternal life, where you will dwell with Him in Heaven forever. His heart's desire is for you to follow and obey Him as He leads you. He wants to lead you so that you can experience His presence regularly. Salvation is the starting point to making the Lord your Shepherd. The concept of the Lord as your loving and personal Shepherd is found all throughout the Bible. However, it seen so beautifully in the popular Psalm 23.

King David, whom I sometimes refer to as the Psalmist, wrote Psalm 23 under the divine inspiration of God.

> *The Lord is my shepherd; I shall not want.*
> *He maketh me to lie down in green pastures: he*
> *leadeth me beside the still waters.*
> *He restoreth my soul: he leadeth me in the paths of*
> *righteousness for his name's sake.*
> *Yea, though I walk through the valley of the shadow*
> *of death, I will fear no evil: for thou art with me;*
> *thy rod and thy staff they comfort me.*
> *Thou preparest a table before me in the presence of*
> *mine enemies: thou anointest my head with oil;*
> *my cup runneth over.*
> *Surely goodness and mercy shall follow me all the days*
> *of my life: and I will dwell in the house of the*
> *Lord for ever.*
>
> — Psalm 23:1–6

Now, let's look at verse 1 of Psalm 23 a little closer. The chapter opens by revealing that God has to be your starting point in order to have a great life. This is why King David begins with the words "The Lord." The King James Bible sometimes capitalizes all the letters of the word "Lord," so I will capitalize them in the same way when quoting Scriptures that do and when making references in certain situations.

The Hebrew word for "LORD" in this verse is *YHWH* (3068), which is the name of God meaning Lord, Jehovah, Yahweh, the Self-Existent One, or the Eternal One. The Hebrew name of God denotes His personal relationship with mankind through salvation. In other words, God wants a personal relationship with His creation. That is why the Lord wants to be your Shepherd. He is not a God who resides far off in a distant land and who cannot be reached or experienced. He is a close God, a personal God. Again, the God who created everything and everyone desires to have a relationship with His creation. *Wow!* Let that really sink in for a moment.

King David says in verse 1 that the Lord "is." When you are reading the psalm, you might not even pause to notice this one little word. However, the word "is" in this case is a powerful word. It serves as a reminder of God's present tense. This verb is not a past-tense or a future-tense verb, but a right-now verb tense. The Lord is here and now. Many Christians pray for something, believing that eventually, down the road or someday in the future, God will answer or come through. Yes, sometimes you do have to wait for the proper season, but many times God wants to move right now. He wants you to have faith right now because faith is a now thing and because God is a now God.

Notice in verse 1 the personal pronoun "my," which indicates David's acceptance of the Lord's desire to be close to His creation. I chose the word "acceptance" carefully because it is the Spirit of God who draws each of us, but it is the individual who must accept the Holy Spirit's tug on their heart. David had a connection with God. David had a special relationship with Him because he did not say that He was "a shepherd" or "one shepherd" or "some shepherd." He said that the Lord was "my" Shepherd.

The words chosen by the Psalmist in verse 1 reveal Psalm 23 as a "conditional" chapter. Do not expect to receive any blessing or promise from Psalm 23 if you do not first have a personal relationship with God through Jesus Christ. The rest of the passages simply will not apply to you. Most of the Bible is conditional, in the sense that you must choose to follow and obey God's Holy Word in order to receive the promises He has for you. God does clearly say that He will always love you unconditionally, and that means no matter what. However, that does not mean you can sin and do anything you want. Yes, God will always love you, but He will always hate sin, which is why you need forgiveness. He will not force you to receive His love, His forgiveness, and His blessings. You must choose to receive all these things. You also must choose to meet the conditions of salvation to receive the blessing of experiencing the presence of God regularly.

Once you meet the condition of salvation that is only found through Jesus Christ, you will be able to say, "the Lord is my Shepherd." The Hebrew word for "Shepherd" is *ra'ah* (7462), which means shepherd, tend, feed, or associate with. God is clear that He wants to associate with you, lead you, and take care of you in every way. He wants to speak with you. He wants to have a relationship with you. He wants to have fellowship with you. He wants to have a friendship with you. The God who created everything wants to be directly involved with you. He wants to lead you into His overflow of blessings on earth and into eternal life in Heaven. But first, you must start by making Him your Shepherd because only He knows the way to blessings, or overflow, on earth and the way to eternal life. Only He can reveal His presence to you.

You cannot experience His presence on your own because the Good Shepherd is the One who leads you to the place where He will reveal Himself. The Shepherd has shown me a pathway to this end, and I am excited to show you in turn. However, you must make God your Shepherd first, or the pathway I show you will not work. The way to make the Lord your Shepherd, to find true rest, and to begin the salvation process is to repent, confess, and accept Jesus Christ as your Lord and personal Savior. I am excited to take you through that process shortly.

The Lord Is My Shepherd

In 1998 when I was fifteen, I began to slowly drift away from God. One night, when I was on my way back home after hanging out with friends, I felt something tell me to put on my seat belt. Before I knew it, I was in a bad car accident. I asked the EMT if I was going to live as I was being rushed to the hospital. The EMT plainly said, "I don't know." I was bleeding profusely from a face trauma. The hospital did a CT scan of my head, and then I was put in a dark, quiet room while they called my family in.

As I lay in that hospital room, I noticed that God was speaking to me. It was not an audible voice, but a still, small voice that was pressing on my heart and mind. It was hard to explain, but I knew it was God. God was knocking on the door of my heart, and He wanted me to let Him in all the way.

Behold, I stand at the door, and knock: if any man
hear my voice, and open the door, I will come in to
him, and will sup with him, and he with me.
— Revelation 3:20

God started speaking to me, telling me that if I would have died, I would have gone to Hell because I had turned my back on Him. That may sound like God was being harsh, but He was not. God told me in such a loving way that it caused me to want to change and be fully committed to Him like never before. I told God that if He would spare me, I would serve Him all the days of my life. In the stillness of that hospital room, all alone, I repented, confessed, and accepted Jesus Christ as my Lord and personal Savior.

The doctor came back into the room to further examine me. The doctor said I could have died instantly based on the way my face struck the car on impact. He said I would need to see a plastic surgeon for reconstructive surgery on my nose and face. The doctor called my survival a miracle. I knew it was an act of God that I was alive. God spared me, saved me, and finished His healing work in me. My body healed in such a great way that I have never had to have any kind of reconstructive surgery.

After my car accident, I started going to church again like never before. I went with my grandparents, with friends, with anyone else who would go, and by myself. I tried my best to be there whenever the doors were open. On April 7, 1999, at the age of sixteen, during a Wednesday night youth church service, I felt God speak to me directly again. God pressed on my heart and mind that I was called to preach. I knew it was God speaking to me again.

I hurried home that night to tell my mother the good news. She gave me the advice not to tell anyone but to wait and see if God really was calling me to minister. Shortly after that, evangelist and senior pastor Rev. Ralph Farmer asked me when I was going to preach for him at his church. That same day, a musician named R. B. Fallen asked me when I was going to preach. I asked R. B. how he knew that I was called to preach. R. B. smiled and said, "I can just tell." I knew that God used Rev. Ralph Farmer and R. B. Fallen to confirm my calling.

On May 14, 1999, at Rev. Ralph Farmer's church in North Fairfield, Ohio, I preached my first sermon to a packed country church with 105 people in attendance. The sermon was titled "Trust." It lasted twelve minutes. One person repented, confessed, and accepted Jesus Christ as their Lord and personal Savior. It was evident to everyone in attendance that I was truly called by God to preach. From that point on, ministers from all denominations began to contact me about preaching at their churches. Rev. Ken Gifford, a local minister, took me under his wing and helped to mentor me in a variety of areas regarding ministry. I continued to minister and grow in the faith, and I soon began my Christian studies. I was ordained in 2003, at the age of twenty, by Ripley Chapel, a nondenominational church. I became an interdenominational evangelist, filling in for all denominations, spreading the Good News of Jesus Christ.

The Lord Your Shepherd

Do you need and want to repent, confess, and accept Jesus Christ as your Lord and personal Savior? Maybe you already are a Christian, but do you want to rededicate your life to Him?

If you are not a Christian, or you already are a Christian but you still want to rededicate your life to Him, this is what you need to know and do:

A. WE HAVE ALL SINNED.

For all have sinned, and come short of the glory of God.

— Romans 3:23

The Greek word for "sinned" is *hamartano* (264), which means sinned, sin, miss the mark, or wrong. The idea is that all of this has been done toward God and against God.

B. GOD LOVES EVERYONE.

For God so loved the world, that he gave his only begotten Son, that whosoever believeth in him should not perish, but have everlasting life.

— John 3:16

C. GOD WANTS EVERYONE TO GO TO HEAVEN.

The Lord is not slack concerning his promise, as some men count slackness; but is longsuffering to us-ward, not willing that any should perish, but that all should come to repentance.

— 2 Peter 3:9

D. JESUS CHRIST IS THE ONLY WAY TO HEAVEN.

Jesus saith unto him, I am the way, the truth, and the life: no man cometh unto the Father, but by me.

— John 14:6

E. YOU MUST REPENT, CONFESS, AND ACCEPT JESUS CHRIST AS YOUR LORD AND PERSONAL SAVIOR.

From that time Jesus began to preach, and to say, Repent: for the kingdom of heaven is at hand.

— Matthew 4:17

That if thou shalt confess with thy mouth the Lord Jesus, and shalt believe in thine heart that God hath raised Him from the dead, thou shalt be saved.

— Romans 10:9

For whosoever shall call upon the name of the Lord shall be saved.

— Romans 10:13

F. TODAY IS THE DAY OF SALVATION!

(For he saith, I have heard thee in a time accepted, and in the day of salvation have I succoured thee:

behold, now is the accepted time; behold, now is the day of salvation.)

— 2 Corinthians 6:2

G. YOU CAN REPENT, CONFESS, AND ACCEPT JESUS CHRIST AS YOUR LORD AND PERSONAL SAVIOR BY PRAYING OUT LOUD AND BELIEVING IN YOUR HEART THE FOLLOWING PRAYER, WHICH IS KNOWN AS THE PRAYER OF SALVATION. YOU CAN PRAY THIS ANYWHERE, ANYTIME, AND WITH ANYONE AROUND:

Dear Heavenly Father,

I confess and I believe that Jesus Christ died on the cross for my sins, and on the third day, You raised Him from the dead. I confess and I accept Jesus Christ as my Lord and personal Savior. I invite Jesus into my heart and into my life. I ask You, God, to forgive me of all my sins, and I forgive everyone. I ask You to save me, help me, change me, and give me a home in Heaven. I ask all of this in Jesus' name. Amen.

Congratulations! The Lord is now your personal Savior. You have started the salvation process. You are a child of God. You are redeemed. You are born again. You are saved. You are a Christian. You are in God's sheepfold because He is your Shepherd. Get baptized. Love Him and your neighbors, live for Him, grow in the faith, follow Him, and obey Him. Daily spend time alone with God seeking Him. Daily pray to God in the name of Jesus. Daily read your Bible. Regularly attend a Bible-believing church. You will be blessed.

Now that you are a Christian and following and obeying Him, He is your Shepherd. You do not need to keep repeating the Prayer of Salvation. However, sometimes it is nice to pray this prayer as a way to rededicate your life to God. Do your best to no longer sin. However, if and when you do sin as a Christian, be quick to repent and confess your sin by asking God to forgive you in the name of Jesus, and He will (1 John 1:9). Learn from your sin so that you do not repeat it. Ask God in the name of Jesus to help you *not* repeat it, and He will. Repenting and confessing your sin will clear the channel between you and God so that you can seek God and experience His presence. Seeking God is a tremendous way to experience the presence of God. Seeking God will help you to draw closer to God and His Kingdom. You can pray for God to help you make sure you are right with Him and to help you seek Him, and He will. Also, every night before you go to bed, even if you have not sinned and have forgiven everyone, still ask God to forgive you of all your sins and forgive everyone. Always make sure there is no unconfessed sin in your life and that you have forgiven everyone. You want to always have a right relationship with God. You want to always be able to hear God clearly. You want to always be ready to experience His presence when He is ready to reveal Himself.

On the pathway to experience God's presence, you have completed the first, and most important biblical step, of salvation. You have the spiritual rest that the Shepherd promised. Make it a habit every day to get to know God in a deeper way by regularly spending time seeking Him. Seeking God regularly will set you up to experience His presence regularly. This time must become a significant part of your life. Let God lead you and be willing to follow and obey. God will lead you to His blessings of overflow on this earth and to His eventual blessings of eternal life in Heaven. You may have already experienced His presence in this first biblical step. I encourage you to go on to the next biblical step, if the Lord leads you, because He may reveal Himself in a new way to you. Do not worry if God has not revealed Himself to you yet because it is coming. What a blessing of God!

Prayer

Dear Heavenly Father,
*   Please help me never to turn my back on You.*
Please help me to grow closer to You every day so I can
experience all that You have for me. I know I cannot
do anything without Your help. May all this be done
for Your glory alone. I ask all of this in Jesus' name.
Amen.

Declaration of Faith

God, I thank You for taking me into Your fold. From this moment on, I know I will experience all the great things You have for me as You lead me forever.

DEVOTIONAL 2

Alone with God

But thou, when thou prayest, enter into thy closet,
and when thou hast shut thy door, pray to thy Father
which is in secret; and thy Father which seeth in secret
shall reward thee openly.

— Matthew 6:6

I remember playing hide-and-seek a lot as a kid. Fast-forward all these years later, and my kids and their friends love hide-and-seek more than anyone I know. They would play every day if they could. Sometimes my wife and I will join in the fun and play with them. I noticed an interesting fact about the game that still has not changed from the time I played as a kid: A vast majority of the people who hide alone do not like to stay hidden for long. They will hide for only about five to ten minutes at most. After that, they get restless, start to move, make sounds, reveal themselves, or team up with others who are hiding. The people hiding simply do not like to be alone for long. However, when it comes to serving God, there is a time to be with people and there is a time to be alone. The Shepherd has given you, His sheep, spiritual rest through salvation. Now it is time to learn the importance of spending time alone with God, which is the second and second-most-important biblical step on the pathway to experiencing His presence regularly.

There is a time to be alone, but there is also a time to be with people. To understand the reason that people generally have a hard time being alone, you must go back to Genesis 1, to the account of God's creation of mankind. Did God need Adam and Eve? *No!* Did God need Adam and Eve to become complete, whole, or satisfied? *No!* He is God. I do not complete Him. You do not complete Him. He is already complete, whole, and satisfied. Why, then, would He create someone in His image?

> *And God said, Let us make man in our image, after*
> *our likeness: and let them have dominion over the*
> *fish of the sea, and over the fowl of the air, and*
> *over the cattle, and over all the earth, and over*
> *every creeping thing that creepeth upon the earth.*
> *So God created man in his own image, in the image*
> *of God created he him; male and female created he*
> *them.*
> *And God blessed them, and God said unto them, Be*
> *fruitful, and multiply, and replenish the earth,*
> *and subdue it: and have dominion over the fish*
> *of the sea, and over the fowl of the air, and over*
> *every living thing that moveth upon the earth.*
> — Genesis 1:26–28

The Hebrew word for "image" is *tselem* (6754), which means image as in a resemblance in regard to an outward form. This means you have outward features just as God also has outward features. God wanted a family that looked like Him and acted like Him, so He created male and female human beings — in His image. God instituted the family unit when

He brought Adam and Eve together and told them to be fruitful and multiply. Notice that the Trinity was at work in this entire process because of the plurality of the words *Us* and *Our* used in verse 26. Furthermore, God showed His desire to have a relationship, fellowship, and friendship with His creation by walking in the cool of the day to talk with His son and daughter (Genesis 3:8). The relationship, fellowship, and friendship you have with God is meant to bring glory to His name (Isaiah 43:7). You were created with the desire for relationship, fellowship, and friendship with the Trinity and with other people.

One of the ways that people have relationship, fellowship, and friendship with the Trinity and with other people is by assembling together as a body of Christian believers. The idea of gathering together to serve God comes from Him. He is clear that Christian believers should not forsake — leave behind — the assembling together while on earth. This is especially true because we are living in the last days, and Jesus could be calling us to Heaven anytime.

> *Not forsaking the assembling of ourselves together, as the manner of some is; but exhorting one another: and so much the more, as ye see the day approaching.*
> — Hebrews 10:25

Different buildings are mentioned in the Bible as places for God's people to gather, fellowship, worship, and learn about Him: temples, tabernacles, synagogues, churches, and homes. Most Christians today — including me — usually call the building and the gathering together of Christian believers a "church." Church denominations are not a bad thing, but each of the denominational titles were started by man. The gathering together of believers was instituted by God.

The word "church," found in Ephesians 5:23, comes from the Greek word *ekklesia* (1577), which means church or a calling out. The idea is that it is a group that has responded to God's call. Therefore, everyone who has repented, confessed, and accepted Jesus Christ as their Lord and personal Savior is part of God's Church. Jesus Christ is the head of the Church (Ephesians 5:23). In Acts 7:38, the Israelites were referred to as "the church in the wilderness" because God had called them out. The Church in Heaven is called the "church of the firstborn" (Hebrews 12:23). Church, the gathering together of believers, can be held anywhere where there are at least two Christians gathered together, led by the Holy Spirit, in the name of Jesus.

> *For where two or three are gathered together in my*
> *name, there am I in the midst of them.*
> — Matthew 18:20

The Greek word for "gathered" is *sunago* (4863), which means gathered, convened, or led together. The idea is that the Spirit of God must be the One to lead two or more Christians together in the name of Jesus in order for Jesus to be there. Believers can gather in Jesus' name anywhere the Lord leads them. They do not have to be in a church three times a week for fifty-two weeks a year. You are not in trouble if you miss church, are scheduled to work on Sunday, or leave town on a vacation. Remember, the Bible says "not forsaking," which means to leave behind in the sense of doing away with. There are also shut-ins, many who cannot drive, and others who simply cannot make it to the church building to gather with other believers because they are ill. For this reason, Christians should make house visits when led by God because He will be in the midst of them when Christians assemble in Jesus' name. God is loving and understanding. However, let me be clear: You should gather with your brothers and sisters in the Lord regularly if you are physically able to do so, and a church building is a great place to accomplish this. Many churches offer different days and times for services to help fit different work schedules and other family obligations. Make sure you make the effort to gather with other believers as often as possible. Also, take your children to church, because it is promised that they will continue to serve God when they are older, if you train them in the ways of God when they are younger.

> *Train up a child in the way he should go: and when*
> *he is old, he will not depart from it.*
> — Proverbs 22:6

Gathering together at a church is not a chore; it is a blessing. Some of my greatest times of experiencing God's presence has happened while at church. My television, radio, and social media ministry is designed to be a supplement to church attendance and to feed those who truly cannot make it to regular church services. Assembling with other believers and worshiping God together is one of the many wonderful blessings we will experience when we finally dwell in Heaven (Psalm 23:6; Revelation 7:15). The will of God is for us to gather with other believers. However, the Bible also clearly shows there is a time to be alone with God, away from people.

God wants you to routinely get away from people to spend time alone with Him. Why? This may be the question you are asking since I just told you how natural and important it is to be social. Let's say that your family are Christians who attend church regularly, where they worship the Lord, hear the Word of God, and have fellowship. At home, your family may read the Bible and pray together, or they may read the Bible and pray in close proximity. Your family is blessed as a result, and your family is growing in the Lord. So, why would you then need to spend time alone with God?

The reason that spending time alone with God is the second and second-most-important biblical step on the pathway, after salvation, is because this is the way God sets everything up for you to go to Him and for you to be heard by Him. In due time, while you are alone, He will come to you and you will be greatly blessed as a result. In other words, once you are alone with God, the atmosphere is set up the way God wants it to be so you can meet with Him. You are starting the process of the special meeting that will take place between you and Him. These special meetings are the best way to grow in the Lord, where you can experience the presence of God regularly. Also, being alone with Him shows your obedience, because that is what Jesus told us to do before we get ready to pray. During this alone time, this is where your praying to God eventually starts. However, I will talk more about the important biblical step of prayer in the next devotional message because that is biblical step three on the pathway. For now, know that your Heavenly Father is in a secret place, you are supposed to imitate and follow Him (Ephesians 5:1), and so now it is time to be alone with Him. Jesus, your greatest example, shows you more on this important topic in His first sermon, which is called the Sermon on the Mount.

> *But thou, when thou prayest, enter into thy closet,*
> *and when thou hast shut thy door, pray to thy Father*
> *which is in secret; and thy Father which seeth in secret*
> *shall reward thee openly.*
>
> — Matthew 6:6

Jesus says, "Enter into thy closet, and when thou hast shut thy door, pray to thy Father which is in secret." The Greek word for "closet" is *tameion* (5009), which means closet, secret chamber, or inner room. He is telling you that God wants you to go into a room for privacy, where you are alone with Him. Then shut the door to talk with Him. Shutting the door furthers the idea of privacy and keeping everyone else out but you and the Lord. The Greek word for "secret" is *krupto* (2927), which means secret, conceal, private, hidden, or inward. He is telling you that the Father is hidden and can be found in private. This part of verse 6 can be summarized in this way: Spend time alone with God by shutting everything else out and then pray to Him who is hidden and who has also shut everything out.

God wants you to be alone with Him, and He wants your time alone to be free from distractions. He desires to spend quality time with you in order to build a deeper relationship, fellowship, and friendship with you. Being free from distractions helps accomplish all this. Another way to look at this is that He is not bringing anyone else with Him to His special meeting with you. He is not bringing anything else to distract Him. He is by Himself, and you have His full, undivided attention. He wants to hear from you. He is coming just for you. How beautiful that is! You also need to come to this special meeting alone, with the understanding that you are coming to meet and speak with the God of all creation. That means you should not bring anyone else with you — *no one*. Not your spouse, not your child, and not your friend. You need to be free from distractions. That means you should put the phone down, setting it on silent mode, turn off the television, turn off the radio, and turn off the computer. You may even turn down or shut off the lights. Anything that is distracting you must be addressed. Let the Holy Spirit lead you as to when is the best time for you to be alone with Him, where to be alone, and how to be alone. Then follow and obey His leading.

Being alone with God is one of the best ways to fully give yourself to God. It helps to fulfill the Scripture which asks you to present your body as a living sacrifice to Him, which is essential to experiencing the presence of God.

> *I beseech you therefore, brethren, by the mercies of God,*
> *that ye present your bodies a living sacrifice, holy,*
> *acceptable unto God, which is your reasonable*
> *service.*
> *And be not conformed to this world: but be ye trans-*
> *formed by the renewing of your mind, that ye*
> *may prove what is that good, and acceptable, and*
> *perfect, will of God.*
> — Romans 12:1–2

You need to present your body as a living sacrifice, yielding yourself to Him. You do this by going alone to God and saying to Him, "Here I am. Not my will be done, but Your will be done." This will help you to crucify your flesh (Galatians 5:24). This will help you to deny yourself, take up your cross, and follow Him (Matthew 16:24). This will help you to seek first the Kingdom of God and His righteousness (Matthew 6:33). Presenting your body as a living sacrifice will help you to be ready to know God's will and experience the presence of God.

Many people in the Bible were alone with God when they experienced His presence. Jacob was alone with God when He wrestled with the Lord (Genesis 32:24). Moses was alone with God when he directly conversed with Him (Exodus 24:2). Daniel was alone with God when he saw a spiritual vision (Daniel 10:8). Elijah was alone with God when he received a revelation and commission from the Lord as God spoke to him in a still, small voice (1 Kings 19:9–18). The high priest would go alone before God once a year, on the Day of Atonement, to offer sacrifices for everyone (Leviticus 16; Hebrews 9:6–7). Thankfully, Jesus Christ became your once-and-forever perfect sacrifice through the shedding of His blood so that you could be saved (Hebrews 9:22; 10:12; John 3:16) and spend time alone with Him regularly. Jesus also spent time alone with His Heavenly Father regularly.

Jesus is the greatest example of why you should spend time alone with your Heavenly Father. Jesus did, and so should you. It is noted in all four Gospels that Jesus took the time to be alone to pray. One time in particular, Jesus had just healed the sick and miraculously fed a multitude of over five thousand people with just five loaves and two fishes. Then He went up into a mountain to pray alone.

And straightway Jesus constrained his disciples to get into a ship, and to go before him unto the other side, while he sent the multitudes away.
And when he had sent the multitudes away, he went up into a mountain apart to pray: and when the evening was come, he was there alone.

— Matthew 14:22–23

Notice that Jesus went to be alone to pray after performing multiple miracles. He was showing you several reasons for praying alone, but I will concentrate on three reasons. First, it shows His humility: He was not seeking recognition because He was praying alone (Matthew 6:5–6). Second, this time alone is when He received messages from the Father of what to do and say (John 5:19; John 12:49). Third, He was showing that this time alone was part of the secret to His power and success in His ministry: He says He can do nothing by Himself without His Father and the Holy Spirit (John 5:19; John 3:34; Acts 10:38). The Holy Spirit was present during these alone meeting times with God because the Trinity does not act independently (Luke 9:34–36; Luke 3:21–22). Therefore, whenever I talk about you being alone with God and experiencing God's presence, know that the complete Trinity is always present. The Trinity always acts in unity. After Jesus had just spent time alone with God the Father and God the Holy Spirit, He immediately moved in power again, by walking on water (Matthew 14:25). Jesus experienced the presence of God and the Holy Spirit over and over, as a result of spending time alone. Being alone with God will help you to be humble, go deeper in the Lord, have power and success in Him, and cause you to experience the presence of the Trinity.

I love going into my prayer closet to be alone and free from distractions with my Heavenly Father. When I was first saved and first became a preacher, the bathroom was my prayer closet. I have a large family, and that was the only place I could be alone where it was quiet. I now call my bedroom my prayer closet. Whether you call it a prayer closet, a prayer room, a secret room, or a secret chamber, it does not matter. Your prayer place may be your bedroom, your bathroom, or a chapel; it does not matter where it is. It just matters that you are alone with God and free from all distractions. I have experienced the presence of God regularly in my prayer closet because I make time alone with God a priority.

I know life is busy, but you must make it a priority to schedule time to be alone with Him. I look forward to being alone with God. It is not a task, it is not difficult, and it is not burdensome. Rather, it is restful, easy, and a relief. I find myself wanting to spend more and more time with God alone. I try to do this at least once a day, and sometimes multiple times a day, because it has helped me tremendously to have a deeper relationship with God. I have had many wonderful times of fellowship with Him as a result. I have also been blessed to have God reveal Himself to me over and over. It is the best part of my day.

Do you spend time alone with God regularly? I hope this devotional message spoke to your heart and mind and gave you the desire to do so. You need to spend time alone with God. He loves to have you experience His presence by speaking to your heart and mind when you are alone with Him. You can pray for God to help you spend time alone with Him, and He will. It may seem like God is playing a game of hide-and-seek, as if God has been hiding and choosing not to reveal Himself.

If so, I ask you, have you made spending time alone with God regularly a priority? If not, then it may seem like God is hiding because He likes to be sought (Isaiah 45:15). He hides in the sense that He has not yet revealed Himself to you. Spending time alone with God and seeking Him is a tremendous way to find Him and experience His presence. God wants you to diligently seek Him. He wants to be sought and desired. He wants to be wanted. God is a jealous God (Exodus 34:14) in the sense that He does not want to share you with anyone or anything else. He loves you first (1 John 4:19), and He wants you to love Him first. He is a God who wants a relationship with you, wants to have fellowship with you, and wants to have a friendship with you. He is waiting for you to get alone and talk with Him. Start today. He will eventually reveal Himself to you.

On the pathway to experience God's presence, you have completed the first, and most important biblical step, of salvation. You have completed the second, and second-most-important biblical step, of spending time alone with God. You have God's full attention, and He has yours, because you are spending time alone with Him. As I mentioned earlier, God can manifest Himself to you in a group setting, but I have noticed that He does it more often when you are alone with Him. I heard a minister once say that you cannot have fellowship with God and humanity at the same time. I think there is a lot of truth in that. Make it a habit every day to spend time alone with God. Spending time alone with God regularly will set you up to experience His presence regularly. This time must become a significant part of your life. Let God lead you and be willing to follow and obey. You may have already experienced His presence in this second biblical step. I encourage you to go on to the next biblical step, if the Lord leads you, because He may reveal Himself in a new way to you. Do not worry if God has not revealed Himself to you yet because it is coming. What a blessing of God!

Prayer

Dear Heavenly Father,
Please help me to spend time alone with You every day. Please clear my path and let nothing hinder or steal this time. I know I cannot do anything without Your help. May all this be done for Your glory alone. I ask all of this in Jesus' name. Amen.

Declaration of Faith

God, I thank You for leading me to a quiet place of rest, where I can be with You alone every day.

DEVOTIONAL 3

Pray

And when he had sent the multitudes away, he went up into a mountain apart to pray: and when the evening was come, he was there alone.

— Matthew 14:23

I remember my mother coming home after every elementary parent-teacher conference and saying the same thing to me: "Your teacher says you are doing great, but you ask a lot of questions." Of course, this was probably a little annoying at times for the teachers. It now brings a smile to my face because I did ask a lot of questions when I was in school. I learned by asking questions until I could grasp the concept I was studying to the fullest. I now laugh because our eldest son, Ricky, is the same way. His teachers have made the same comments about him. He also asks me a ton of questions about God, which I love. I still have many questions, but now they are primarily for God. I take my questions to Him in prayer as I seek to know Him and His ways more. I have taught Ricky, our other son, Riley, and our daughter, Vera, that they can ask my wife and me anything. Also, I have taught them that they can take any questions they might have to God in prayer because He loves to talk with them. God wants to talk with you and answer any questions you have. The Shepherd has given you, His sheep, spiritual rest through salvation, and you are spending time alone with God. Now it is time to learn the importance of praying, which is the third biblical step on the pathway to experiencing the presence of God regularly.

Countless books have been written on the subject of prayer. I will highlight in this devotional message some of the deeper points on the topic of prayer that will help you as you seek to experience God's presence. Before I start highlighting these deeper points, there are three general points to keep in mind and practice every time you pray. These three general points are the foundations of prayer that you must practice and understand to go deeper. Of course, I am assuming you are a Christian and you are spending time alone with God. The first general point is to let the Holy Spirit lead you and help you because you cannot pray effectively without Him. As I have already mentioned, He is the Good Shepherd who leads His sheep. The Holy Spirit will lead you concerning when to pray, where to pray, and how to pray. If you do not know what to pray yet, wait quietly for the Holy Spirit to speak to your heart and mind because He is known as the Spirit of prayer (Zechariah 12:10). It is important to pray in the Spirit (Ephesians 6:18). Follow and obey His leading in every area of your life, including in the area of prayer.

> *For as many as are led by the Spirit of God, they are the sons of God.*
>
> — Romans 8:14

> *Likewise the Spirit also helpeth our infirmities: for we know not what we should pray for as we ought:*

but the Spirit itself maketh intercession for us with
groanings which cannot be uttered.

— Romans 8:26

The second general point is that you must believe, have faith, and not waver in that faith.

But let him ask in faith, nothing wavering. For he
*   that wavereth is like a wave of the sea driven*
*   with the wind and tossed.*
For let not that man think that he shall receive any
*   thing of the Lord.*
A double minded man is unstable in all his ways.

— James 1:6–8

God knows what you have need of before you ask (Matthew 6:8). However, He wants you to ask because it is a powerful way to release your faith (James 4:2; Proverbs 18:21; Hebrews 11:6). There will be times when you are struggling to believe, have faith, and not waver. It is okay to pray and ask God to help you in your areas of unbelief, and He will (Mark 9:17–27). Seek Jesus and you will receive faith because He is the Author of faith (Hebrews 12:2). Your faith will also grow as you hear from God and study His Word (Romans 10:17). Your faith will grow as you establish your relationship with the Trinity.

The third general point is to be humble when you pray (Matthew 6:5–6), because God promises to lift up the humble (James 4:10). After all, you cannot even pray on your own. Humble yourself by being alone with God when you pray and remembering how much you need Him. Cry out to Him and tell Him that if He does not answer, it will not happen. There may be times when you need to humble yourself by fasting. Combining prayer and fasting is a powerful weapon to defeat the devil and his demons (Matthew 17:21). Humble yourself by telling God the Father, God the Son, and God the Holy Spirit how much you need Them.

First you must practice these three general points about prayer every day, but you must also go a little deeper on this topic of prayer, because I want God to reveal His presence to you. The reason that prayer is the next biblical step on the pathway, after spending time alone with God, is because that is what Jesus did. It says in Matthew 14:23 that Jesus sent the multitudes away and went up into the mountain where He was alone. What did He do next? *Pray.* This was literally the next thing He did. It was the reason He sent the multitudes away. He needed to have a special meeting with His Father and the Holy Spirit. Jesus knew that praying to God while alone would cause His prayers to be answered.

> *But thou, when thou prayest, enter into thy closet,*
> *and when thou hast shut thy door, pray to thy Father*
> *which is in secret; and thy Father which seeth in secret*
> *shall reward thee openly.*
>
> — Matthew 6:6

Jesus says, "Thy Father which seeth in secret shall reward thee openly." The Greek word for "seeth" is *blepo* (991), which means seeth, perceive, or take heed. The idea is that God sees something in the physical realm, and it impacts the spiritual realm. The Greek word for "secret" is *krupto* (2927), which is the same word used earlier in the verse. It means secret, conceal, private, hidden, or inward. The idea is that the Father sees what is done in private, in secret. In other words, He sees what you do when you are alone. The Greek word for "reward" is *apodidomi* (591), which means reward, deliver again, repay, or recompense. The idea is that God is going to give back to you what is rightfully yours, what belongs to you as His child. He is going to answer your prayer. This part of verse 6 can be summarized this way: God sees what you are doing alone in the physical realm, and it will impact the spiritual realm, causing your prayers to be answered. Now let me summarize all of verse 6 together for you: Spend time alone with God by shutting everything out. Next, pray to Him who is hidden and who has also shut everything out. God will see you alone praying, thus causing the spiritual realm to be stirred, and your prayers will be answered.

You now understand to be alone and pray, just like Jesus did. However, you may be asking, "What is prayer?" Prayer is simply talking with God. Talking about what? Well, *anything*. More specifically, prayer can be seen as *asking* something of God. First Samuel 1 talks of a woman named Hannah who wanted a child. Hannah sought God for a child as she desperately prayed, vowed, and wept before Him. One of the best biblical definitions of *prayer* is found when Hannah was asking God for a child:

> *And Hannah answered and said, No, my lord, I am a woman of a sorrowful spirit: I have drunk neither wine nor strong drink, but have poured out my soul before the LORD.*
>
> — 1 Samuel 1:15

The Hebrew word for "poured out" is *shaphak* (8210), which means poured out, pour out, gush out, cast out, or spill forth. The Hebrew word for "my soul" is *nephesh* (5315), which means my soul, desire, passion, emotion, appetite, life, or living being. Your soul can be called your mind, will, and emotions. It is what you think, want, and feel. It can also be described as your personality. It is the battleground of the flesh (body) and spirit. To summarize, Hannah earnestly poured out her soul to God because she was asking for her heart's desire. And guess what? God answered. Hannah gave birth to a child named Samuel. And afterward, she kept her promise and dedicated him to the Lord, and he became a great prophet of God.

Jesus talks a lot about prayer the first time He preaches, in the sermon known as the Sermon on the Mount. He teaches that talking with God and asking God for our needs and wants are important parts of prayer. He shows this in the most beautiful example of what a model prayer looks like, which is known as the Lord's Prayer.

> *After this manner therefore pray ye: Our Father which art in heaven, Hallowed be thy name.*
> *Thy kingdom come, Thy will be done in earth, as it is in heaven.*
> *Give us this day our daily bread.*
> *And forgive us our debts, as we forgive our debtors.*
> *And lead us not into temptation, but deliver us from evil: For thine is the kingdom, and the power, and the glory, for ever. Amen.*
> — Matthew 6:9–13

Later in the Sermon on the Mount, Jesus reiterates the importance of asking things from God. He goes on to say that God will give you exactly what you are asking for.

Ask, and it shall be given you; seek, and ye shall find;
knock, and it shall be opened unto you:
For every one that asketh receiveth; and he that
seeketh findeth; and to him that knocketh it shall
be opened.
Or what man is there of you, whom if his son ask
bread, will he give him a stone?
Or if he ask a fish, will he give him a serpent?
If ye then, being evil, know how to give good gifts
unto your children, how much more shall your
Father which is in heaven give good things to
them that ask him?

— Matthew 7:7–11

You now understand that praying is talking to God and asking. However, you may be wondering how to pray. Prayer is so simple. You pray by asking God for anything you need and want and then ending the prayer by saying "in the name of Jesus," and your prayer will be answered.

And in that day ye shall ask me nothing. Verily, verily,
I say unto you, Whatsoever ye shall ask the Father in
my name, he will give it you.

— John 16:23

And whatsoever ye shall ask in my name, that will I
do, that the Father may be glorified in the Son.

If ye shall ask any thing in my name, I will do it.

— John 14:13–14

You should always pray to God because He is your Heavenly Father. You pray by asking God for anything, and I will explain this in further detail later. Then you end the prayer by asking for it to be done in the name of Jesus. You ask in the name of Jesus because that is the source of power and authority. This is known as the Christian's "power of attorney." The power of attorney is a legal concept that refers to someone giving you permission to conduct business on their behalf and by their authority using their name. Jesus gives you permission to conduct business on His behalf and by His authority using His name. As a child of God, everything you say and do, including prayer, should be done in the name of the Lord Jesus (Colossians 3:17).

You already understand the importance of going alone before God because He will see you in your secret place and will answer. You already understand that prayer is talking with God and specifically asking. You already understand that prayer is done by asking God anything in the name of Jesus. Now, when you are alone and want to pray, how do you begin? You start to pray by asking God for His forgiveness and by forgiving everyone. Yes, I know you are already a Christian if you have repented, confessed, and accepted Jesus Christ as your Lord and personal Savior. I covered this in the first devotional in this book, concerning salvation, when I explained how to be saved. You do not need to go through the Prayer of Salvation again. However, you still need to first come to Him by His blood, which was shed for the remission of sins (Hebrews 10:19; Matthew 26:28). If there is iniquity in your heart, He will not hear your prayers (Psalm 66:18). Therefore, first begin your prayer time by asking God for His forgiveness of all non-hidden and hidden sin (Psalm 139:23–24). Then make sure you forgive everyone.

> *For if ye forgive men their trespasses, your Heavenly*
> *   Father will also forgive you:*
> *But if ye forgive not men their trespasses, neither will*
> *   your Father forgive your trespasses.*
> — Matthew 6:14–15

> *But if we walk in the light, as He is in the light, we*
> *   have fellowship one with another, and the blood of*
> *   Jesus Christ His Son cleanseth us from all sin.*
> *If we say that we have no sin, we deceive ourselves,*
> *   and the truth is not in us.*
> *If we confess our sins, he is faithful and just to*
> *   forgive us our sins, and to cleanse us from all*
> *   unrighteousness.*
> — 1 John 1:7–9

Once you have confessed your sins by asking God for His forgiveness and you have forgiven everyone, you are cleansed from all unrighteousness by the blood of Jesus. You can now pray about the things that concern you and God. You will have the peace of knowing there is nothing between you and Him, so your prayers will be heard and will not be hindered. Also, you will know that your prayers for others will be heard and will not be hindered because you have made sure first that you are right with God in every way (Matthew 7:3–5).

You are now ready to pray to God in the name of Jesus about the things that concern you and God. Prayer beautifully takes you deeper in the Lord because you are drawing even closer to Him and His Kingdom by talking with Him. You can pray by asking God to help you with your needs (Matthew 6:8). This is not a hard concept for you to grasp as you have probably asked for God to help you physically, with a job, and whatever other personal needs you may have. You have probably prayed for your children, family, friends, and co-workers as part of your needs. Of course, you pray for them because you love them, but also this can be part of your own needs because their lives and decisions can affect you. God will answer as He promises to supply all your needs (Philippians 4:19).

God says that you can also pray for more than just your needs. You can pray about your wants (Psalm 23:1; 34:9–10; 3 John 2) and all things (Matthew 21:22; Mark 11:22–24). You can ask for anything (John 14:14; 1 John 5:14), and you can ask for whatsoever (Matthew 21:22; John 14:13; 15:16; 16:23; 1 John 3:22). All of this language of the Bible shows that every area of your life is covered. You can pray asking for anything and everything. It does not get clearer than that. I cover this particular subject much more in my book *Psalm 23: A Psalm for the Living.*

The idea that God puts no limits on what you can ask Him for frightens many people for some reason. I think people worry that others or themselves are going to become greedy in their prayers. Therefore, it is not often taught how the Bible says you can ask for what you want. However, if the Holy Spirit is helping you to pray, you will not become greedy in your prayers. I have come up with three questions that you can use to help determine whether you are praying properly as you pray about your needs, your wants, all things, anything, and whatsoever. If you can answer "yes" to all three of these questions about what you are praying for, then you can rest assured knowing it is a prayer that God will answer in due season. God will never go against these three questions. I call these questions *The Prayer Test*.

The Prayer Test

1) DOES YOUR REQUEST COMPLETELY AGREE WITH THE BIBLE?

God cannot lie. He has always been and always will be in perfect and complete harmony with the Bible. Therefore, make sure your prayer completely agrees with the Word of God.

> *In hope of eternal life, which God, that cannot lie, promised before the world began.*
>
> — Titus 1:2

> *In the beginning was the Word, and the Word was with God, and the Word was God.*
>
> — John 1:1

> *All scripture is given by inspiration of God, and is profitable for doctrine, for reproof, for correction, for instruction in righteousness.*
>
> — 2 Timothy 3:16

2) IS YOUR REQUEST A GOOD THING?

God is a good God who only does good things. Therefore, make sure your prayer is asking for something good.

> *O taste and see that the Lord is good: blessed is the man that trusteth in him.*
>
> — Psalm 34:8

> *Every good gift and every perfect gift is from above, and cometh down from the Father of lights, with whom is no variableness, neither shadow of turning.*
>
> — James 1:17

3) DOES YOUR REQUEST GLORIFY GOD?

You were created for the glory of God. Everything you do should glorify God. It is the Lord's desire that the earth be filled with His glory. Therefore, make sure your prayer brings glory to God.

> *Even every one that is called by my name: for I have created him for my glory, I have formed him; yea, I have made him.*
>
> — Isaiah 43:7

> *Whether therefore ye eat, or drink, or whatsoever ye do, do all to the glory of God.*
>
> — 1 Corinthians 10:31

But as truly as I live, all the earth shall be filled with the glory of the Lord.

— Numbers 14:21

Maybe you are still struggling with what to pray. Remember to let the Spirit of God lead you by waiting on Him and letting Him lay something on your heart and mind. Then use *The Prayer Test* to make sure it is from God, because God will never do anything that goes against those three questions. Your prayer does not need to be long, and it does not need to have repetitions (Matthew 6:7). Keep it simple. Come humbly but boldly before Him, and be honest with Him (Hebrews 4:16; Psalm 51:6). Pray regularly by making it a habit because God is waiting for you. The Lord's Prayer is a beautiful and simple prayer to pray anytime, but it is especially great to pray when you do not know what to pray.

I have experienced God's goodness firsthand as a result of prayer. It has been said that God's phone number is Jeremiah 33:3. I call God's phone number a lot, and He answers.

Call unto me, and I will answer thee, and shew thee great and mighty things, which thou knowest not.

— Jeremiah 33:3

I can say with certainty that God has been better to me than I have been to Him. I can summarize God's goodness to me by saying that He has always answered every prayer I have ever prayed — in His way and in His timing. Sometimes there is a waiting season, but He always comes through. For the prayers He did not answer exactly like I had prayed, He ended up doing something greater than what I was believing for. I have learned to also pray about the blessings He has given me. God has blessed me with the privilege of being a television minister, interdenominational evangelist, senior pastor, and author. The fact that God uses me for His glory is a result of God's goodness to me. I continue to pray about these areas of ministry, as I follow and obey His leading to reach the lost, edify the saints, and minister to people of all ages and in all walks of life for the glory of Jesus Christ.

Do you pray to God regularly? I hope this devotional message spoke to your heart and mind and gave you the desire to do so. You need to pray to God. He loves to have you experience His presence by speaking to your heart and mind when you pray to Him. You can pray for God to help you pray, and He will. The Good Shepherd wants you to experience His goodness firsthand as a result of your prayers. First, make sure you are praying every day. If you are praying and your prayers are not being answered, go back and reread this devotional message to see if God speaks to you about something that will help you. Then follow His leading and obey. Do not be afraid to ask God for good things. You can experience His goodness every day (Psalm 23:6). Ask Him to bless your family, your church, your co-workers, your neighbors, and even your enemies. Ask Him for anything and everything, seek Him, and knock by continually praying (Matthew 7:7; 1 Thessalonians 5:17). God wants to rain His abundant goodness into your life, so be willing to receive it. He promises to not withhold any good thing from those who walk uprightly (Psalm 84:11). After God answers a prayer, give Him thanks, praise, and worship. Declare His glory and let your light shine by sharing your testimonies with others about what God has done.

On the pathway to experience God's presence, you have completed the first, and most important biblical step, of salvation. You have completed the second, and second-most-important biblical step, of spending time alone with God. You have completed the third biblical step of praying. You have access to everything that God has for you through the power of prayer. Make it a habit every day to pray to God in the name of Jesus. Praying to God regularly will set you up to experience His presence regularly. This time must become a significant part of your life. Let God lead you and be willing to follow and obey. You may have already experienced His presence in this third biblical step. I encourage you to go on to the next biblical step, if the Lord leads you, because He may reveal Himself in a new way to you. Do not worry if God has not revealed Himself to you yet because it is coming. What a blessing of God!

Prayer

Dear Heavenly Father,

Please help me to pray the way You would have me to pray. Please answer all my prayers quickly in the supernatural and let me receive them in the natural now. I know I cannot do anything without Your help. May all this be done for Your glory alone. I ask all of this in Jesus' name. Amen.

Declaration of Faith

God, I thank You for answering all of my prayers.

DEVOTIONAL 4

Thanksgiving

*Be careful for nothing; but in every thing by prayer
and supplication with thanksgiving let your requests
be made known unto God.*

— Philippians 4:6

My wife, Victoria, and I recently took our kids on a much-needed vacation. We had a great time relaxing and soaking up the Florida sun while enjoying the beautiful scenery. It was one of those vacations that we did not want to end. However, the thing that blessed Victoria and me the most was something our kids did. Multiple times, out of nowhere, and without being prompted, they thanked us for taking them on the trip. Our kids have always been grateful kids, but they went above and beyond on that vacation to show how grateful they were. The way they expressed their gratitude touched our hearts in a special way that caused us to want to do even more for them. Just like our kids being thankful moved us, when we as the children of God are thankful to our Heavenly Father, God pours out His blessings on us. The Shepherd has given you, His sheep, spiritual rest through salvation, you are spending time alone with God, and you are praying. Now it is time to learn the importance of thanksgiving, which is the fourth biblical step on the pathway to experiencing the presence of God regularly.

The reason that thanksgiving is the next biblical step on the pathway, after prayer, is because that is what the Bible mentions after prayer. In the opening verse of this devotional message, Philippians 4:6, it says that you are to pray with "thanksgiving." The Greek word for "thanksgiving" is *eucharistia* (2169), which means thanksgiving, thankfulness, gratitude, grateful, or giving thanks. The thanksgiving this verse is talking about is giving God thanks because of the gratitude you have for all that He has done and all that He will do. Also, you give God thanks because He is good and because of His goodness towards you (1 Chronicles 16:34; Ephesians 5:20).

Thanksgiving is oftentimes tied to prayer because giving thanks is an expression of your faith. You may pause while you are praying to give God thanks and then go back to praying. However, it is very important to give God thanks after you pray because it powerfully releases more of your faith concerning everything you just prayed about. You are giving God thanks because you know He is accomplishing great things in the spiritual realm and that the manifestation of answered prayers is soon to follow. Thank God for dispatching His angels to answer your prayers (Psalm 103:20–23; Daniel 10). Giving thanks helps you to remain in faith until your prayers are manifested in the natural, with answers that you can see. Therefore, giving thanks for what you are asking for is the simplest way to express your faith.

The Bible talks a lot about thanksgiving in connection with prayer. Daniel, a great prophet of God, prayed three times a day and then gave thanks to God after praying.

Now when Daniel knew that the writing was signed,
he went into his house; and his windows being open
in his chamber toward Jerusalem, he kneeled upon his
knees three times a day, and prayed, and gave thanks
before his God, as he did aforetime.

— Daniel 6:10

Daniel's regularity in being alone with God, praying, and giving thanks gave him power and favor with God. This is why God promoted him, used him for His glory, and stopped the mouths of hungry lions that would have devoured him. God loved the way Daniel handled himself so much that God divinely inspired him to write his own book of the Bible. If Daniel gave thanks after praying, so should you and I.

Jesus gives a beautiful example of the connection between prayer and thanksgiving in John 11. It is a story that I have preached many times because there are so many godly nuggets of information in it. I will paraphrase this powerful story for you: A man named Lazarus, who was the friend of Jesus, was sick to the point of death. Lazarus's sisters, Mary and Martha, sent word to Jesus that their brother needed His healing touch. Jesus stayed in the nearby place where He was staying and did not move. Lazarus died, and then Jesus came to Lazarus's home after Lazarus had already been dead for four days. Jesus wept for His dead friend and went to his grave, where He had them remove the stone from the tomb. Jesus then prayed with thanksgiving to God as an expression of His faith, and Lazarus was raised from the dead.

*Then they took away the stone from the place where
the dead was laid. And Jesus lifted up his eyes, and
said, Father, I thank thee that thou hast heard me.
And I knew that thou hearest me always: but because
of the people which stand by I said it, that they
may believe that thou hast sent me.
And when he thus had spoken, he cried with a loud
voice, Lazarus, come forth.
And he that was dead came forth, bound hand and
foot with graveclothes: and his face was bound
about with a napkin. Jesus saith unto them, Loose
him, and let him go.*

— John 11:41–44

Jesus gives you a beautiful example of what to do if you want to see a miracle. He prayed and gave thanks, both with faith. Notice that He gave thanks for both what God had done and what He was going to do. Then, Jesus raised Lazarus from the dead by the power and might of His spoken word. Jesus is your greatest example, and He took the time to give God thanks with His prayers. The result speaks for itself. Follow the example of Jesus to witness life-changing miracles by giving thanks to God with your prayers.

Giving thanks is so important to Jesus that He notices when you do not give thanks. I will summarize this important fact that is found in Luke 17:11–19: Jesus entered a village where ten men who had leprosy, a horrible skin disease, asked Jesus to have mercy on them. In other words, they asked for healing. Jesus told them to go and show themselves to the priest, and as they went, they were healed. When one of them noticed they had been healed, he turned back and started glorifying

God. Then he fell down at Jesus' feet and gave Him thanks. However, Jesus noticed that the other nine did not come back to give thanks.

> *And Jesus answering said, Were there not ten cleansed? but where are the nine?*
>
> — Luke 17:17

All ten leprous men were praying by asking Jesus for a healing touch. But only one gave thanks after their prayer, which means that only 10 percent were thankful in this particular story. Jesus was obviously not happy that only one of them came back to give thanks. I wonder what percentage of Christians take the time to be thankful to God, Jesus, and the Holy Spirit. I wonder if it is only 10 percent. A lady once came to my church asking for prayer because she had just found out she had serious lung cancer. Our congregation prayed for her, and I felt the Lord tell me she was healed. She went to her appointment that same week, and they did a final screen so they could get everything set up for her cancer treatments. The screening came back and showed the cancer was completely gone. It was a miracle of God. She let me know the good news, and we all rejoiced with her. The sad thing is, she never came back to church, and she never went to another church that I am aware of. Sure, she gave thanks, but then she stopped serving God. God wants your thanks, and He wants you to continue to serve Him.

Like all the other previous biblical steps, let the Holy Spirit lead you and help you as to when to give thanks, where to give thanks, and how to give thanks. You cannot even give God thanks without His help. Giving God thanks helps prepare you later for praise and worship. I will talk about praise and worship in upcoming devotional messages, but the pathway God has shown me to experience God's presence has you give thanks before praise and worship.

> *Enter into his gates with thanksgiving, and into his courts with praise: be thankful unto him, and bless his name.*
>
> — Psalm 100:4

The Hebrew word for "gates" is *shaar* (8179), which means gates, gate, or door. The gate is the way into a place. It is oftentimes surrounded by a wall or a fence. You can think of the gate as an entrance to God's Kingdom. A gate, along with a wall or fence, is used to keep out those who are unwelcome. Heaven has gates with a high wall, and the only way to enter is through Jesus Christ.

> *And had a wall great and high, and had twelve gates, and at the gates twelve angels, and names written thereon, which are the names of the twelve tribes of the children of Israel.*
>
> — Revelation 21:12

> *Jesus saith unto him, I am the way, the truth, and the life: no man cometh unto the Father, but by me.*
>
> — John 14:6

I think the first thing that everyone who makes it to Heaven will do is start thanking God that they made it. That will be the very first thing that I do! Then I will start running with praise to God's throne, where I will bow down in worship before Him. Even now, when you enter a church, you should start thanking God. Thank God for the privilege and honor it is to come to His house. Giving God thanks oftentimes leads to praise and then worship. You can think of the pathway as a process of drawing closer to God and going deeper in His Kingdom as you seek Him. Salvation is the starting point in your relationship with God the Father, God the Son, and God the Holy Spirit. You are in God's family, and you are drawing closer to Him and His Kingdom. Being alone draws you closer to God, and you are at the gate of His Kingdom. Everything is set up for a special meeting between you and the Lord. Praying draws you closer to God, and you see the opening of the gate of His Kingdom. You are talking with the Lord. Thanksgiving draws you even closer to God, and you enter through the gate of His Kingdom. You thank the Lord because your heart is so full of gratitude that you have entered in.

I will be the first to admit that I used to not be as thankful as I should have been. I know one could say that you can never give God all the thanks that is due His name, and that is true. It was not that I was ungrateful; it was that I just did not take the time to give God thanks like I should have. This biblical step on the pathway has really changed my life. It has made me stop and take the time to give God thanks for all the little things and for all the big things. I now make it a priority to give God thanks for what He has done and for what He is going to do. I understand that giving thanks is powerful enough by itself to make miracles happen (John 6:1–13). I love to release my faith through thanksgiving. I even have a list in my phone of the numerous things that God has done for me. This way, if I ever feel like I am struggling to be thankful, I can use that list to remind me of the abundance of testimonies that God has given me. My list is continually growing.

I want to be thankful to God the way our kids were thankful to us for taking them on vacation. We cherish how they just randomly and sincerely kept telling us "thank you." It brought smiles to our faces and our hearts. I want to make sure there are numerous times when I just randomly stop and say "thank You" to God, Jesus, and the Holy Spirit. I want to make my Heavenly Father smile because I love Him, and I am grateful for everything He has given me.

Do you give God thanks regularly? I hope this devotional message spoke to your heart and mind and gave you the desire to do so. You need to give God thanks. He loves to have you experience His presence by having you physically feel His power when you thank Him. You can pray for God to help you give thanks, and He will. Quickly become a thankful person by giving God thanks after you pray. I encourage you to make a list like I have, so on days when you are alone in your quiet time praying and you may not be feeling thankful, you can take your list out and be reminded of what God has done for you. It will be so uplifting to you as you read from your list. Your faith will be released as you speak thanksgiving to God. By doing so, you will definitely put a smile on God's face.

On the pathway to experience God's presence, you have completed the first, and most important biblical step, of salvation. You have completed the second, and second-most-important biblical step, of spending time alone with God. You have completed the third biblical step of praying. You have completed the fourth biblical step of giving thanks. You have gone even deeper in God as you are now through the gates and offering thanks to Him. Make it a habit every day to give thanks to God. Thanking God regularly will set you up to experience His presence regularly. This time must become a significant part of your life. Let God lead you and be willing to follow and obey. You may have already experienced His presence in this fourth biblical step. I encourage you to go on to the next biblical step, if the Lord leads you, because He may reveal Himself in a new way to you. Do not worry if God has not revealed Himself to you yet because it is coming. What a blessing of God!

Prayer

Dear Heavenly Father,

Please bring to remembrance all that You have done for me so that I can glorify You in a way that pleases You. I know I cannot do anything without Your help. May all this be done for Your glory alone. I ask all of this in Jesus' name. Amen.

Declaration of Faith

God, I thank You for helping me to give You thanks in all things.

DEVOTIONAL 5

Praise

Enter into his gates with thanksgiving, and into his courts with praise: be thankful unto him, and bless his name.

— Psalm 100:4

Most people thoroughly enjoy going to a celebration. After all, most celebrations take place because of a joyous occasion. Most people get all cleaned up, and possibly even dressed up, because it is considered a special event. It is a moment that brings many people together. I have given speeches and invocations, and I have officiated many celebrations. The celebrations of which I have been a part have been for church events, high school halls of fame, college halls of excellence, college commencements, Chamber of Commerce events, and weddings, to name a few. All these events have something in common: People are collectively celebrating the accomplishments of an individual, a couple, or a group. The fact that you attend says that the recipients are worthy or have done something that should be commended. I always enjoy attending our local college hall of excellence, where they recognize the accomplishments of three local business leaders each year. The college makes a video about each individual summarizing their childhood, business accomplishments, and their current endeavors. The videos showcase the reasons these individuals are worthy of notable distinction. In other words, they share the great things they have accomplished. Someday you and I will be invited to the biggest celebration ever in Heaven, which praises God the Father, God the Son, and God the Holy Spirit for who They are and for all the great things They have accomplished. However, you do not have to wait until Heaven to start celebrating Them. The Shepherd has given you, His sheep, spiritual rest through salvation, you are spending time alone with God, you are praying, and you are giving thanks. Now it is time to learn the importance of praise, which is the fifth biblical step on the pathway to experiencing the presence of God regularly.

The reason that praise is the next biblical step on the pathway, after giving thanks, is because that is what the Bible says to do. In the opening verse of this devotional message, Psalm 100:4, it says that after you give thanks, you are to go "into His courts with praise." The Hebrew word for "courts" is *chatser* (2691), which means courts, court, yard, or village. The Hebrew word for "praise" is *tehillah* (8416), which means praise, song of praise, deep place, depth, or hymn. The Hebrew word *tehillah* (8416) originates from another Hebrew word for "praise," *halal* (1984), which means praise, glorify, celebrate, commend, shine, make a show, or boast. This part of verse 4 can be summarized in this way: Praise draws you even closer to God, and you enter the courtyard of His Kingdom. You praise God because you see His majesty and glory as you draw so close to His throne.

When most people think of praising God, they think of singing. Yes, singing is one of the greatest ways to praise God (Hebrews 2:12). However, you can also just speak your praise to God without it having to be in the form of a song. Psalm 150, in six short verses, teaches some more very important and interesting points about praise. It shows that God desires praise from people on earth and from those in Heaven (verse 1). It says the reason you are to praise God is because of His mighty acts and excellent greatness (verse 2). It says you can praise Him with instruments and dance (verses 3–5). It concludes by saying that if you have breath, you should praise the Lord (verse 6). No doubt, this is the most fitting way to end the book of Psalms, which is the hymnbook of the nation of Israel.

> *Praise ye the LORD. Praise God in his sanctuary:*
> *praise him in the firmament of his power.*
> *Praise him for his mighty acts: praise him according to*
> *his excellent greatness.*
> *Praise him with the sound of the trumpet: praise him*
> *with the psaltery and harp.*
> *Praise him with the timbrel and dance: praise him*
> *with stringed instruments and organs.*
> *Praise him upon the loud cymbals: praise him upon the*
> *high sounding cymbals.*
> *Let every thing that hath breath praise the LORD.*
> *Praise ye the LORD.*
>
> — Psalm 150:1–6

The fact that everyone and everything should praise God is found in Psalm 148. Angels, sun and moon and stars, animals, weather, mountains, trees, and people are some of the things commanded to praise God in Psalm 148. God is worthy to receive glory and praise because He created everything

(Colossians 1:16). His intention was that everything He made, both in the heavens and on earth, should declare the glory of God by praising Him (Psalm 19:1; 148; Numbers 14:21).

Psalm 148:2 tells the angels to praise Him. The angels did this so beautifully at the birth of Jesus Christ.

> *And suddenly there was with the angel a multitude of*
> *the heavenly host praising God, and saying,*
> *Glory to God in the highest, and on earth peace, good*
> *will toward men.*
>
> — Luke 2:13–14

The angels in Heaven praise God. The Bible also talks about angels worshiping God in Heaven. I will talk more about worshiping God in the next devotional message, because worship is to be done as you draw even closer to God.

By now you understand that praising God is vital. He desires it, and He deserves it. Now let me show you the power of praise, and how to use it as a weapon (2 Corinthians 10:4). First you need to understand who you are fighting. I remember as a young minister not understanding how a Christian could call any person an enemy. I thought only the devil and his demons could be our enemies. As I grew in the faith, the Lord led me to understand that people will also be our enemies at times. The difference is with whom you wrestle.

> *For we wrestle not against flesh and blood, but*
> *against principalities, against powers, against the*
> *rulers of the darkness of this world, against spiritual*
> *wickedness in high places.*
>
> — Ephesians 6:12

The Greek word for "wrestle" is *pale* (3823), which means wrestle, fight, or have conflict. Therefore, when you wrestle and fight, it is only to be against the devil and his demons, not against flesh and blood. Jesus says that you do not fight against the people who are your enemies, but instead you are supposed to show them love.

> *Ye have heard that it hath been said, Thou shalt love*
> *thy neighbor, and hate thine enemy.*
> *But I say unto you, Love your enemies, bless them that*
> *curse you, do good to them that hate you, and pray*
> *for them which despitefully use you, and persecute*
> *you;*
> *That ye may be the children of your Father which is in*
> *heaven: for he maketh his sun to rise on the evil*
> *and on the good, and sendeth rain on the just and*
> *on the unjust.*
> — Matthew 5:43–45

The Greek word for "enemy" is *echthros* (2190), which means enemy, adversary, hated, or hostile. Jesus is saying that people will hate you and will be hostile toward you. The devil will even use people to come against you in a variety of ways. However, you cannot hate the *people*, retaliate, wish them ill, or wrestle against them. Instead, you must love them, bless them, and pray for them. I now understand that I will have enemies who are physical and spiritual in nature, but I only may fight against the demonic. If a person comes against me as an enemy, I must act the right way toward them. However, I will be looking for the devil and his demons behind that person, which is whom I will fight.

The weapon of praising God is a strong weapon to silence the devil and release the power of God.

Out of the mouth of babes and sucklings hast thou ordained strength because of thine enemies, that thou mightest still the enemy and the avenger.

— Psalm 8:2

The Hebrew word for "strength" is *oz* (5797), which means strength, praise, might, boldness, or power. The idea is that praise defeats our enemies. Jesus also shows the fact that praise is part of the meaning when He quotes this verse in Matthew 21:16. Notice something else interesting: Psalm 8:2 uses the words *enemies*, *enemy*, and *avenger*. The word *enemies* can refer to anyone, spiritual or physical, who is an adversary against you. Therefore, this includes any physical person who is being used by the devil and his demons as a tool to be your enemy. Remember, you fight the devil and his demons behind the person — you do not fight the person. The word *enemy* refers to your main adversary, which is the devil. The word *avenger* can refer to an enemy, spiritual or physical, who is looking to take vengeance against you. Therefore, this includes any physical person who is being used by the devil and his demons as a tool to be an avenger towards you. Again, you fight the devil and his demons behind the person — you do not fight the person. One of the ways to defeat your spiritual enemies, the devil and his demons, is to praise God. If a physical enemy is coming against you, one of the ways to defeat the devil and his demons behind the person, is to praise God.

Powerful things happen when you take time to praise God. He does mighty acts and is the most powerful Person. The praises of God go up, and the power of God comes down. The power of prayer accompanied by praise is what caused Paul and Silas to be set free from prison (Acts 16:25–26). Praise went up and setting-free power came down. The power of praise causes the spirit of heaviness to leave (Isaiah 61:3). Praise goes up, and demonic spirits have to leave. I regularly use the power of praise to defeat all the enemies that come against me, because I know that as praise goes up, miracles come down.

I am the furthest thing from a singer, and I have no musical talent at all, so singing a song to praise God does not come naturally to me. I remember one time when I was a young minister visiting a church, they asked if anyone had a special song to sing. Immediately, God laid on my heart that I should sing a hymn called "I'll Fly Away." I argued with God a little in my mind because I am a horrible singer, and He knows this. I finally gave in and raised my hand, telling them I had a song to sing, so they had me come on up to sing. The piano player had been playing her whole life, and she could play anything. She told me that if I would start singing, she would find the right key. So, I started singing. This is where I wish I could tell you the angels of God surrounded me and helped me to sing beautifully. Unfortunately, this did not happen. Instead, the piano player never found my key, and my singing was horrible. The congregation just stared at me, wondering what in the world I was doing. I walked back to the pew with my head down, wondering why God had allowed this to happen. Then a tremendous peace and joy from the Holy Spirit came over me as God told me how happy He was that I had obeyed Him. I jokingly told God to never ask me to do that again, and He never has.

The good news is that the Bible says to make a joyful noise to the Lord, so it does not matter if what you produce sounds good or not (Psalm 100:1). Also, giving God praise has nothing to do with how good of a singer you are or how musically talented you are. It has everything to do with how mighty the acts of God are and how great He is. The focus of praise is on God, not ourselves. I regularly give God praise in my quiet time. Sometimes I will play a song and sing along. Sometimes I will sing to God without a song playing. Sometimes I just simply speak praises to God by declaring His great works and great power. Sometimes I just praise God with one word.

One of my favorite words that I use to praise God is *hallelujah*. That word resonates with me when I sing it, speak it, or hear it. The chorus of "Hallelujah" was popular at many Christian events back in the 1970s. I like to close many of my ministry services by having the crowd stand and sing a chorus of "Hallelujah." The Spirit of God seems to flow in a mighty way when that beautiful word is sung or spoken out to the Lord. In the King James Version of the Bible, Psalm 111:1 starts out by saying, "Praise ye the LORD," which in the Hebrew is the word, *Hallelujah*. Furthermore, *Hallelujah* is made up of two Hebrew words. The first word is *halal* (1984), which means praise, glorify, celebrate, commend, shine, make a show, or boast. The second word is *YHWH* (3068), which means the name *Jah* in reference to Jehovah the Lord. Therefore, saying, "Hallelujah" is like saying, "Hail, God the Creator and Redeemer." No wonder it is so powerful when sung or simply spoken as a praise to God. In addition, Psalms 111–118 are known as the "Hallelujah Psalms."

Do you praise God regularly? I hope this devotional message spoke to your heart and mind and gave you the desire to do so. You need to praise God. He loves to have you experience His presence by having you physically feel His power when you praise Him. You can pray for God to help you give praise, and He will. For some people, it is natural because they love to sing, and they love music. However, remember that praising God truly has nothing to do with singing, how good you can sing, or even using music. It has everything to do with God. Let the praises of God flow out of your heart. Praising God blesses Him and causes Him to move in mighty ways on your behalf. He will silence the devil and those who want to harm you. Once you start praising God more, it will radically change your life for the better. You will look forward to this part of the pathway.

On the pathway to experience God's presence, you have completed the first, and most important biblical step, of salvation. You have completed the second, and second-most-important biblical step, of spending time alone with God. You have completed the third biblical step of praying. You have completed the fourth biblical step of giving thanks. You have completed the fifth biblical step of giving praise. You have gone even deeper in God as you are now in His courtyard, drawing nearer to His throne, and offering praise to Him. Make it a habit every day to give praise to God. Praising God regularly will set you up to experience His presence regularly. This time must become a significant part of your life. Let God lead you and be willing to follow and obey. You may have already experienced His presence in this fifth biblical step. I encourage you to go on to the next biblical step, if the Lord leads you, because He may reveal Himself in a new way to you. Do not worry if God has not revealed Himself to you yet because it is coming. What a blessing of God!

Prayer

Dear Heavenly Father,

Please help me to have a song or word of praise in my heart for You. I want to glorify You and sing of Your wonderful acts and exceeding power. You deserve all the praise, glory, and honor. I know I cannot do anything without Your help. May all this be done for Your glory alone. I ask all of this in Jesus' name. Amen.

Declaration of Faith

God, I thank You for helping me to praise You.

DEVOTIONAL 6

Worship

All nations whom thou hast made shall come and worship before thee, O LORD; and shall glorify thy name.

— Psalm 86:9

One day when I was in my mid-twenties, I was standing in my kitchen, when a pain came over me that literally dropped me to my knees. I cried out for God to help me because I felt like my body was being repeatedly punched, and I felt like vomiting. I then cried out for my wife to help me, not knowing what was going on with my body. She came running and said she would call an ambulance. I told her that I felt like I was dying so she had to take me to the hospital because the ambulance might not make it in time. I crawled out on my hands and knees to the vehicle, and she rushed me to the hospital. I was taken immediately to the emergency room, where they discovered that I only had a kidney stone. The nurse gave me medicine to alleviate my pain. I praised the Lord that it was not anything more serious than a kidney stone. I battled kidney stones on and off for years after that and passed at least eight of them. One day God told me to start drinking two bottles of water a day, so I did, and I still regularly do. I have never had another kidney stone attack after that, and that was years and years ago. I know staying hydrated helps with kidney stones, but I truly believe God healed me and has blessed my obedience. However, I will never forget that day when I fell straight to my knees and cried out for God to help me. I knew that God was the source of my help, and He prevented my ailment from being anything worse. The Bible says that at the name of Jesus every knee should bow (Philippians 2:10). Bowing on your knees is a way to worship God. The Shepherd has given you, His sheep, spiritual rest through salvation, you are spending time alone with God, you are praying, you are giving thanks, and you are giving praise. Now it is time to learn the importance of worship, which is the sixth biblical step on the pathway to experiencing the presence of God regularly.

The reason that worship is the next biblical step on the pathway, after praise, is because you are drawing even closer to God and you come before His throne in His Kingdom. Remember, you can think of the pathway as a process of drawing closer to God and going deeper in His Kingdom as you seek Him. Salvation is the starting point in your relationship with God the Father, God the Son, and God the Holy Spirit. You are in God's family, and you are drawing closer to Him and His Kingdom. Being alone draws you closer to God, and you are at the gate of His Kingdom. Everything is set up for a special meeting between you and the Lord. Praying draws you closer to God, and you see the opening of the gate of His Kingdom. You are talking with the Lord. Thanksgiving draws you closer to God, and you enter through the gate of His Kingdom. You thank the Lord because your heart is so full of gratitude that you have entered in. Praising draws you closer to God, and you enter the courtyard of His Kingdom. You praise the Lord because you see His majesty and glory as you draw so close to His throne. Worshiping draws you even closer to God, and you come before His throne in His Kingdom. You worship the Lord because you are in reverence of His holiness.

To understand worship and its importance, you have to understand from the beginning how worship toward God worked in Heaven. Lucifer, who later became the devil, was a beautiful angel in Heaven that had coverings of precious stones with musical instruments in him (Ezekiel 28:13). He did not need someone else to play an instrument to God because *he himself* was the instrument played to God. The name *Lucifer* shows that he was created for worship to God, because he was called the "son of the morning" (Isaiah 14:12). The Hebrew word for "son of the morning" is *helel* (1966), which means son of the morning, morning star, a shining one, or lucifer. The idea was that he was a light bearer because of his shining presence. It seems like Lucifer, as a light bearer, would reflect the glory of God that shone on him by shining it back to God. These are the main reasons many believe that Lucifer led worship in Heaven. While we are not entirely sure whether Lucifer led worship, it appears as if he did. If Lucifer did not lead worship, he definitely still worshiped God because of his position and because of the musical instruments that were in his very being.

Lucifer decided he no longer wanted to worship God. Instead, Lucifer wanted to be the object of worship. Lucifer became full of the sin of pride, and he convinced one-third of the angels to follow him. Lucifer and his angels then tried to overthrow God. However, God kicked Lucifer and Lucifer's angels out of Heaven to earth. Lucifer and his angels have been trying ever since to get mankind to worship Lucifer (Ezekiel 28:13-19; Isaiah 14:12-15; Revelation 12:3-4).

John 8:44 shows that Lucifer became known as the devil. Revelation 12:9 tells us that he is known as the devil and Satan. The Greek word in John 8:44 and Revelation 12:9 for "devil" is *diabolos* (1228), which means devil, false accuser, or slanderer. The devil is a liar and everything evil. The third of the angels that followed Satan are known in the King James Version of the Bible as "devils" (Mark 16:17), "familiar spirits" (Leviticus 20:6), "unclean spirits" (Mark 1:27), "evil spirits" (Luke 7:21), and "seducing spirits" (1 Timothy 4:1). In Luke 8:29, the Greek word for "devil" and in Mark 16:17 the Greek word for "devils" is *daimonion* (1140), which means devil(s), evil spirit(s), fallen angel(s), or demon(s). This Greek word is where the words *demon* and *demons* come from. Therefore, in our modern language, Satan's angels against whom Christians now fight are primarily called demons. Although the King James Version of the Bible does not use the words *demon* or *demons*, most other translations do. Also, in our modern language, Satan's angels are often called "fallen angels." In summary: devils, familiar spirits, unclean spirits, evil spirits, seducing spirits, and fallen angels can be rightfully called demons. Just like their fallen leader, the devil, demons are liars and everything evil. Demons work with Satan trying to bring all manner of evil against you. Therefore, it is the devil and his demons that are your spiritual enemies. You fight against the devil and his demons because they are trying to stop you from serving and worshiping God (1 Peter 5:8; Ephesians 6:12). Remember, the devil wants your worship, and he will do everything he can to try and receive it. If you are not worshiping God, you are worshiping the devil because there is no in-between (Matthew 12:30).

(*Important to note:* Some Christian circles debate the idea that fallen angels are now demons by pointing to Scriptures in Genesis 6 and elsewhere. Furthermore, some say the Bible does not give a clear account as to where demons come from. However, do not get caught up in that debate. The important thing to note is that the Bible clearly says that demons are real, they work for the devil, they are liars, they are everything evil, and Christians fight against them.)

God took away the dominion of the devil and his demons by creating Adam and Eve and giving them control of the earth. Adam and Eve could worship God directly because there was no sin that separated them from God. Adam and Eve eventually sinned by disobeying God when they were deceived by the devil. As a result of their sin, they gave dominion back to the devil and his demons, and they could no longer directly worship God because their sin separated them from God. Since the shedding of blood has to be made for the forgiveness of sins, animal sacrifices were implemented during the time of the Law to bring people back to a place where they could serve and worship God. Animal sacrifices had to be made frequently because the sacrifices were not good enough or powerful enough to eliminate sin. Animal sacrifices did not give true victory over sin. (Genesis 2:15–3:8; Ephesians 2:2; Hebrews 9:22; Hebrews 10:1–18).

Jesus came to accomplish everything the Law and animal sacrifices could not. Jesus came off His throne, which is at the right of God in Heaven, to come to earth and accomplish His plan to redeem mankind. He did so by being conceived of the Holy Spirit and born through the Virgin Mary. He then shed His perfect and innocent blood on the cross so only His sacrifice was needed. His sacrifice is perfect and powerful enough to entirely cleanse and eliminate sin. His sacrifice gives true victory over sin. God then raised Jesus from the dead on the third day and ensured that He conquered death, Hell, and the grave. Jesus then went back to His position, which is at the right hand of God. Then, God the Holy Spirit came into the world to help you with your Christian walk. He does this by making you born again, comforting you, teaching you, reminding you, convicting you of sin, guiding you, giving you power, making you alive, helping you with your weaknesses, making intercession for you, giving you revelation and wisdom, living in you, giving you spiritual gifts, leading you, setting you apart for God's use, and sealing you. The Trinity works together on everything because They love you. Now, in order to be completely right with God, you must repent, confess, and accept Jesus Christ as your Lord and personal Savior. Follow the Good Shepherd and obey Him. You can now worship God directly because sin no longer separates you from God — you have been washed in the blood of Jesus Christ, and you have true victory over sin through Jesus Christ. (John 3:5–16; Matthew 1; Matthew 27–28; John 14:26; John 16:8–13; Acts 1:8; Romans 8:6–27; 1 Corinthians 2:10–11; 1 Corinthians 6:19; 1 Corinthians 12:7–11; Galatians 5:16–21; Ephesians 1:13).

In the opening verse of this devotional message, Psalm 86:9, it says that God wants everyone to worship Him. That is how important worship is to God. He wants no sin to separate you because He wants all people to come before Him and worship Him. This beautifully ties in with how God created you to glorify Him (Isaiah 43:7; Numbers 14:21). Worship is so important to God that in the Ten Commandments, the first two commandments deal with worship.

1st Commandment:

Thou shalt have no other gods before me.
— Exodus 20:3

2nd Commandment:

Thou shalt not make unto thee any graven image, or
any likeness of any thing that is in heaven above, or
that is in the earth beneath, or that is in the water
under the earth.
— Exodus 20:4

The first and second commandments are different but closely related. You will notice that words like *serving* and *worshiping* oftentimes go hand in hand. Therefore, sometimes I may use both words or just one of the words. The first commandment deals with whom you are to serve and worship as God. In Exodus 20:3, the Hebrew word for "before" is *al* (5921), which means before, upon, or beside. The idea of this verse is that you are *not* to serve and worship anyone or anything but Jehovah God. There is *none* besides Him. He is the only God. Anyone or anything else is a false god. God alone is to be the focus of whom you serve and worship. You are to acknowledge that He is the only true God, so it is Him alone that you serve and worship. The second commandment deals with how you are to worship God. You are *not* to worship God through an idol or graven image or anyone or anything else. In other words, you are only to worship God directly without the use of an idol or graven image or anyone or anything else.

The story of the golden calf in Exodus 32:1–14 shows the Israelites breaking the first and second commandments. Here is a summary of that story: Moses was on the mountain speaking with God. The Israelites became restless and asked Aaron to make a god for them. Aaron gathered golden earrings from the people and made a golden calf. Aaron introduced the calf as a god, and then he made an altar along with it. He then later called the calf LORD, as in Jehovah God. Offerings were then made on the altar before this calf. God told Moses to go back to the people because they had worshiped the calf. God was angry and wanted to destroy the people because of their sins. However, Moses interceded for the people by praying for mercy, and God had mercy and spared them.

Aaron and the children of Israel broke the first commandment of serving and worshiping something other than God Eternal. This was seen when the idol was referred to as "god" (Exodus 32:4). You are only to serve and worship God. They broke the second commandment of worshiping God through an idol. This was seen when the idol was referred to as "Lord" (Exodus 32:5). You are only to worship God, and you worship Him directly without the use of an idol or graven image or anyone or anything else.

Serving and worshiping is serious business, and God created you for both. Therefore, you will serve and worship somcone or something whether you intend to or not. If you are *not* serving and worshiping God, you are serving and worshiping the devil because there is no in-between (Matthew 12:30). You must make the choice to serve and worship God. Serving and worship is to be reserved for God alone (Matthew 4:10). Anyone or anything else you put before God or put too much focus on is what you will serve and worship. People serve and worship people and numerous things, which is the same as serving and worshiping the devil. Remember, there is no in-between. You serve and worship God or the devil. The devil and his demons lay traps through lust, pride, and other temptations that cause many to sin, which causes many to serve and worship wrongfully.

And the cares of this world, and the deceitfulness of riches, and the lusts of other things entering in, choke the word, and it becometh unfruitful.
— Mark 4:19

Choosing rather to suffer affliction with the people of God, than to enjoy the pleasures of sin for a season.
— Hebrews 11:25

If you serve or worship anyone or anything else besides God, it will destroy your life in every way. You will inevitably end up in Hell, so flee from all of this by serving, worshiping, and fearing God alone.

Thou shalt not bow down thyself to them, nor serve them: for I the LORD thy God am a jealous God, visiting the iniquity of the fathers upon the children unto the third and fourth generation of them that hate me.
— Exodus 20:5

And fear not them which kill the body, but are not able to kill the soul: but rather fear him which is able to destroy both soul and body in hell.
— Matthew 10:28

The way to make sure you are serving, worshiping, and fearing God and Him alone is by letting the Holy Spirit lead you. Make sure you seek God, His Kingdom, and His righteousness first so that you stay on His straight and narrow path.

> *But seek ye first the kingdom of God, and his righteousness; and all these things shall be added unto you.*
> — Matthew 6:33

> *Enter ye in at the strait gate: for wide is the gate, and broad is the way, that leadeth to destruction, and many there be which go in thereat:*
> *Because strait is the gate, and narrow is the way, which leadeth unto life, and few there be that find it.*
> — Matthew 7:13–14

Let's focus back in on worshiping God as a Christian. I have already told you how worship draws you even closer to God, and it is like being before His throne in His Kingdom. You are a child of God, you are alone with God, and you have already prayed. You have given thanks and praise with your soul (Psalm 107:1; Psalm 146:1). Although thanks and praise are mainly done in the soul, they can be done in spirit through the Spirit of God because a Christian's spirit is joined with the Holy Spirit as one spirit (1 Corinthians 6:17). As a Christian, your body is a temple of the Spirit of God because He lives inside of you, which is why you are one with the Lord (1 Corinthians 6:19). However, when it comes to worship, it is not done in the soul. Worship is to be done only in spirit and in truth, which is why it is even deeper, and it is like being before the throne of God in His Kingdom.

> But the hour cometh, and now is, when the true wor-
> shippers shall worship the Father in spirit and in
> truth: for the Father seeketh such to worship him.
> God is a Spirit: and they that worship him must
> worship him in spirit and in truth.
>
> — John 4:23–24

The Greek word for "Spirit" and "spirit" is *pneuma* (4151), which means Spirit, spirit, wind, breath, or mental disposition. This further shows the closeness between the Holy Spirit and the Christian's spirit. Man's spirit is considered to be the part that knows (1 Corinthians 2:11). Notice the spirit of man can involve the intellect, mind, and will. So, how do you worship in spirit? This can be hard to explain, as the soul and spirit of a person are intertwined but distinct. It can be hard to differentiate some of the finer details of the soul and spirit. However, it is sometimes differentiated by saying the soul feels and the spirit knows. The soul and spirit both make up the inner person, which makes you alive. The body is the casing that holds the soul and spirit. Once a person dies, the soul and spirit will go either to Heaven or to Hell, depending on whether the person is saved or not (2 Corinthians 4:16-18). The body goes back to dust, and you will later be given a new body that will house your soul and spirit again (Genesis 3:19; Daniel 12:1–2). A child of God will give God thanks, praise, and worship in Heaven. Heaven is full of worship (Revelation 4, 7, 11, 15, 22:9). In Hell, there will be *no* worshiping of Satan, but instead there will be weeping and gnashing of teeth

(Matthew 13:50). Let me explain to you how to worship God on earth.

It is essential to let God lead you in every biblical step of the pathway because they are spiritual biblical steps filled with glorious spiritual experiences. However, it is vital to let the Spirit of God lead you in when to worship, where to worship, and how to worship because worship must be done in spirit and in truth (John 4:24). You need the Good Shepherd's leading more than ever in order to worship the way He would have you to worship. As you move from giving thanks and praise to worship, you can tell when the Spirit of God moves your spirit into worship. You become focused on God in a deeper way. You focus on His holiness and worship Him because of it. You fear Him as you worship Him.

> *O worship the LORD in the beauty of holiness: fear*
> *before him, all the earth.*
>
> — Psalm 96:9

It is as if the Holy Spirit moves your spirit when you focus your entire being on God, who alone is holy (Revelation 15:4). It is hard to describe, but you will know when you are truly worshiping. If you do not know whether you are truly worshiping, then you are probably not. You know because the spirit is the part that knows. It is like you have entered another level of closeness with God. This is where a lot of times you will experience the presence of God, which causes you to physically feel or see a display of His power. I have felt His power come over me many times while I was worshiping Him. What a wonderful way to experience the presence of God.

Just as you worship Him in spirit as the Holy Spirit helps you, you also must worship Him in revealed biblical truths. Here are some of the main biblical truths about worship that will help you worship God in truth:

1. You worship only God (Exodus 20:3).
2. You do *not* use idols or graven images or anyone or anything else to worship God (Exodus 20:4).
3. You worship God because He alone is holy (Psalm 96:9; Revelation 15:4).
4. You worship God by bowing down in the fear of the Lord (Psalm 95:6; 96:9).
5. You worship God by giving yourself to Him (Romans 12:1–2).
6. You worship God by exalting Him (Psalm 99:9).

Again, let the Spirit of God help you worship God. The Holy Spirit may have you exalt God in worship in different ways. One day He may lead you to sing, another day to make declarations of His holiness, another day to play a musical instrument, or another day just to bow in silent reverence. Follow His leading and obey.

I notice the Holy Spirit has me worship God in different ways at different times. Sometimes I speak of His holiness and declare His truths. Sometimes I lie down face-first with my arms outstretched and say nothing. Sometimes I bow on my knees in awe of Him. I do not plan my worship time. Instead, in my alone time, I do what the Holy Spirit is leading me to do. If I do not sense the Holy Spirit is leading in a certain way, sometimes I will simply wait awhile. If I still do not sense His leading, I oftentimes will worship God by singing a song about His holiness. I love to experience the manifestation of His presence by feeling His power as I worship.

Do you worship God in spirit and truth regularly? I hope this devotional message spoke to your heart and mind and gave you the desire to do so. You need to worship God. He loves to have you experience His presence by having you physically feeling His power when you worship Him. You can pray for God to help you worship, and He will. It is great to give thanks and praise. However, worshiping God is so much deeper and more powerful. Give the Holy Spirit the chance to lead you in your worship. You will be amazed as to how He shows up. If you do not sense a certain leading of the Holy Spirit, wait a little while. If you still do not know His leading, exalt God by declaring His holiness. Worshiping Him will change your life for the better.

On the pathway to experience God's presence, you have completed the first, and most important biblical step, of salvation. You have completed the second, and second-most-important biblical step, of spending time alone with God. You have completed the third biblical step of praying. You have completed the fourth biblical step of giving thanks. You have completed the fifth biblical step of giving praise. You have completed the sixth biblical step of worshiping. You have gone even deeper in God, as you are now before His throne in His Kingdom worshiping Him. Make it a habit every day to worship God. Worshiping God regularly will set you up to experience His presence regularly. This time must become a significant part of your life. Let God lead you and be willing to follow and obey. You may have already experienced His presence in this sixth biblical step. I encourage you to go on to the next biblical step, if the Lord leads you, because He may reveal Himself in a new way to you. Do not worry if God has not revealed Himself to you yet because it is coming. What a blessing of God!

Prayer

Dear Heavenly Father,
Please help me to worship You in spirit and in truth. I want the Spirit of God to use me to worship You in a way that is pleasing to You. I know I cannot do anything without Your help. May all this be done for Your glory alone. I ask all of this in Jesus' name. Amen.

Declaration of Faith

God, I thank You for helping me to worship You in spirit and in truth.

Read the Bible

Thy word is a lamp unto my feet, and a light unto my path.

— Psalm 119:105

I remember being in the eighth grade and carrying my Bible everywhere in school. I would read it when I had free time in class, when I was in study hall, while on the bus to my basketball games, and when I got home from school. Typically, I would read ten chapters a day during the week and twenty a day on the weekends. I had a supernatural desire from God to want to read the Bible. I look back now and can see that God was preparing me for ministry, which He called me into at the age of sixteen. Since then, I have read the Bible numerous times from beginning to end and have studied countless subjects in the Bible. I have a master of theology (ThM) degree and a doctor of ministry (DMin) degree because I love to learn about the Word of God. I have a God-given faith to know that everything in the Bible is completely true. God meant what He said, and He said what He meant. I take the Bible as literally as possible. When the Bible uses figurative language, I get the literal message that is being conveyed through the figurative language. The Bible is what I use in every decision to see what is of God and what is not of God. You need to know the

Bible so you can know what is of God and what is not of God. The best way to know the Bible is to read it. The Shepherd has given you, His sheep, spiritual rest through salvation, you are spending time alone with God, you are praying, you are giving thanks, you are giving praise, and you are worshiping. Now it is time to learn the importance of reading the Bible, which is the seventh biblical step on the pathway to experiencing the presence of God regularly.

I prayed and pondered about how to handle this devotional message. Originally, I thought I would prove to you, with historical documents, landmarks, archaeological findings, and science, how the Bible is tried, tested, and true. I could tell you how God orchestrated everything in the Bible and how it perfectly matches countless secular findings. In some ways, this is what Ken Ham, the founder and CEO of *Answers in Genesis*, does through his books, speaking engagements, and museums. I am a huge fan of Ken Ham, and God has used him in mighty ways to prove many biblical truths in various ways. However, the more I prayed and thought about this devotional message, the more I felt God tell me that my focus should be on the *faith* aspect of the Bible to prove the Holy Scriptures. Someone might say that you cannot prove the Bible by quoting from the Bible. My reply to that is, "Yes, you can." Take a step of faith and just simply give God a chance to prove Himself by believing, following, and obeying the Word of God. He will show you. After all, faith is what pleases God (Hebrews 11:6).

I came to the realization, around the age of fifteen, that if I would have faith by believing, following, and obeying God, then He would show and prove Himself to me. One day I was at my high school cross-country practice, thinking and trying to prove God's existence through my own logic, reasoning, and understanding. I was saying that I know there is a God because of this, this, and this. I inserted my own logic and reasoning into this statement. I was leaning on my own understanding — as the Bible tells us not to do.

> *Trust in the LORD with all thine heart; and lean not*
> *unto thine own understanding.*
> *In all thy ways acknowledge him, and he shall direct*
> *thy paths.*
>
> — Proverbs 3:5–6

God lovingly corrected me and told me what to do instead. He spoke to my heart and mind and told me to just believe and let Him do the rest. So, if a doubt or question about the Bible would come up, I would just quote a Bible Scripture and try not to figure it out or worry about it. It worked. All of a sudden, I had a supernatural faith come on me, and it has been with me to this day. I did not realize it at the time, but now I understand that I was doing what Jesus did in Matthew 4:1–11. Here is a summary of what Jesus did: The devil came three times to tempt Jesus, trying to get Him to sin. The devil was lying and twisting the Word of God. Jesus did not get into a debate, He did not argue, and He did not use human logic, reasoning, or understanding. Instead, every time Jesus said, "It is written." Then Jesus would quote the Word of God. It defeated the devil. I now understand that I was defeating the devil the same way as Jesus without realizing it. It worked. I do the same thing now, and it still works.

Releasing your faith by speaking the Word of God will defeat the devil and glorify God. There will be times when you are struggling to believe, to have faith, and to not waver. Your faith will grow as you hear from God and His Word (Romans 10:17). It is okay to pray and ask God to help you in your areas of unbelief, and He will (Mark 9:17–27). Here are some of the main Scriptures God has used to help me with my faith in the Word of God, to know the Bible is for me and is true. Study these Scriptures, meditate on them, believe them, put them into practice, and quote them, and you will be blessed.

1) THE WORD OF GOD EXISTED FROM THE BEGINNING, AND GOD DIVINELY INSPIRED MEN TO WRITE IT DOWN. THESE WRITINGS BECAME KNOWN AS THE BIBLE. THE TRINITY WALKS IN PERFECT HARMONY WITH THE BIBLE, AS SHOWN BY JESUS BEING CALLED THE WORD.

In the beginning was the Word, and the Word was with God, and the Word was God.

— John 1:1

2) ALL SCRIPTURE IS FROM GOD AND IS PROFITABLE FOR YOU.

And that from a child thou hast known the holy scriptures, which are able to make thee wise unto salvation through faith which is in Christ Jesus.
All scripture is given by inspiration of God, and is profitable for doctrine, for reproof, for correction, for instruction in righteousness:
That the man of God may be perfect, thoroughly furnished unto all good works.

— 2 Timothy 3:15–17

3) GOD THE FATHER, GOD THE SON, AND GOD THE HOLY SPIRIT LOVE YOU.

For God so loved the world, that he gave his only begotten Son, that whosoever believeth in him should not perish, but have everlasting life.

— John 3:16

4) YOU ARE A CHILD OF GOD BECAUSE YOU HAVE REPENTED, CONFESSED, AND ACCEPTED JESUS CHRIST AS YOUR LORD AND PERSONAL SAVIOR. THEREFORE, YOU HAVE ALL HIS PROMISES.

For ye are all the children of God by faith in Christ Jesus.

— Galatians 3:26

5) ALL THE PROMISES AND BLESSINGS GIVEN TO ABRAHAM AND ISRAEL BELONG TO YOU BECAUSE YOU ARE THE SEED OF ABRAHAM THROUGH SALVATION IN JESUS CHRIST.

And if ye be Christ's, then are ye Abraham's seed, and heirs according to the promise.

— Galatians 3:29

6) ANYTHING THAT GOD HAS DONE FOR SOMEONE ELSE, HE WILL DO FOR YOU, BECAUSE HE DOES NOT SHOW FAVORITISM.

For there is no respect of persons with God.
— Romans 2:11

The reason that reading the Bible is the next biblical step on the pathway, after worship, is because it is time for you to draw even closer to God, prepare for what He is calling you to do, and have the knowledge and power you need to succeed. You just were at the throne of God, deep within His Kingdom, drawing closer to Him through worship. I know you do not want to leave His feet because it is so glorious and the feeling of His power is tremendous. However, reading the Bible will draw you even closer to God because you are continuing to learn about Him. Reading the Bible will prepare you for what God would have you to do. Reading the Bible will give you the knowledge and power you need to succeed in every situation you will face. It is time to have faith in the Bible, read the Bible, and study the Bible. God is a God of action. He has a plan that you must go and fulfill — so He will be sending you out. Therefore, I want to focus on how you must read your Bible so that you will be prepared.

The Great Commission

The disciples had just finished worshiping Jesus when God gave them a call to action, which is known as the Great Commission. You have just finished worshiping Jesus, and you will now be receiving a call to action. Start preparing by reading the Word of God.

> *Then the eleven disciples went away into Galilee, into*
> *a mountain where Jesus had appointed them.*
> *And when they saw him, they worshipped him: but*
> *some doubted.*
> *And Jesus came and spake unto them, saying, All*
> *power is given unto me in heaven and in earth.*
> *Go ye therefore, and teach all nations, baptizing them*
> *in the name of the Father, and of the Son, and of*
> *the Holy Ghost:*
> *Teaching them to observe all things whatsoever I have*
> *commanded you: and, lo, I am with you always,*
> *even unto the end of the world. Amen.*
> — Matthew 28:16–20

Notice that after worshiping, God gave them the instructions of the Great Commission, which is fourfold:

1) "GO YE THEREFORE" (VERSE 19)

The first thing Jesus tells them is to "go." This command is for every believer. God wants the whole world to be saved (John 3:16), and we all have a job to do for God because He has a plan for everyone (Jeremiah 29:11). You should go as God gives you direction and go with the abilities that He has given you. Let the Holy Spirit lead you as always.

2) "TEACH ALL NATIONS" (VERSE 19)

The Greek word for "teach" is *matheteuo* (3100), which means teach, make a disciple, or disciple. The idea is to help someone to progressively learn the Word of God by enrolling them as a student to become a disciple. The key is that they are to become disciples so they can then help others to become Christians and then disciples. You are to make disciples of all nations.

3) "BAPTIZING THEM IN THE NAME OF THE FATHER, AND OF THE SON, AND OF THE HOLY GHOST" (VERSE 19)

Baptism is a way of declaring publicly that you are a follower of Jesus. Therefore, you can baptize those who become saved from any nation. Baptize them in the name of the Father, Son, and Holy Ghost. Baptizing others may be out of your comfort zone, but Jesus gives you the right and authority to do so. Let God lead you to baptize others in His perfect way and timing.

4) "TEACHING THEM TO OBSERVE ALL THINGS WHATSOEVER I HAVE COMMANDED YOU" (VERSE 20)

The Greek word for "teaching" is *didasko* (1321), which means teaching, teach, direct, impart knowledge, instruct, or admonish. The idea is to instruct someone so they can learn. The key is that they are to learn the ways and things of God, which He commands through His Word. You are to teach all nations.

In order to fulfill the Great Commission, you need to know the Word of God. God wants you to be a witness for Him (Isaiah 43:10–12). He wants you to tell others how much Jesus loves them (John 3:16) and how to be saved (Romans 10:9). He wants you to help others. In order to accomplish all of this and everything else God wants you to do, you need to know the Bible. After all, it has the answer to every question and problem, and it holds the keys to experiencing the presence of God. Reading the Bible daily is the best way to learn the Word of God. Furthermore, I recommend every day reading a portion of it out loud because it is powerful when you speak it (Proverbs 18:21).

The ministries the Lord has blessed me with have experienced tremendous growth. I am honored to be His child and humble servant. As the ministry has grown, I receive countless prayer requests regularly. My wife and I love to release our faith and agree in prayer for the power of God to answer all the prayer requests received. We pray according to God's Word as the Holy Spirit leads. In other words, when a prayer request comes in, we find out what the Bible says about that request, and then we pray according to His Word. For example, when someone requests prayer for a healing touch of their body, we know the Bible says in Isaiah 53:5 that by the stripes of Jesus we are healed. So, we know it is God's will for healing to take place. Therefore, we agree in prayer by asking God for a healing touch to take place in the name of Jesus for the person who had the request. Glory be to God; He hears all our prayers and loves to answer them. People are saved, healed, delivered, blessed, and have experienced other miracles. Also, as the ministry has grown, I receive many questions about God. I provide people with the answers to their questions by using the Bible as the Holy Spirit leads me. The answer to every question and problem can be found in the Bible. I love the Word of God, and I believe it wholeheartedly, as I have seen the power and results it delivers. In the opening verse of this devotional message, Psalm 119:105, it says that God's Word illuminates the way. Let it illuminate your way.

Do you read the Bible regularly? I hope this devotional message spoke to your heart and mind and gave you the desire to do so. You need to read the Bible as part of the pathway. God loves to have you experience His presence by speaking to your heart and mind as you read His Word. You can pray for God to help you read the Bible, and He will. You need to know the Bible so that all your questions and problems can be answered and solved, and so you can help others by knowing what advice to give them and what to pray for them. It is the living Word of God, and it has all your answers. There is nothing wrong with hospitals, doctors, nurses, lawyers, counselors, etc., but go first to the Word of God for your answers. Do not waste valuable time looking for your answers and trying to figure out how to handle situations when God has the answers for you in His Word. Let the Spirit of God lead you in every way as to where to read and how much to read. Maybe you should start in the New Testament in the book of Matthew. Maybe you should read just one verse or one chapter. Again, let the Holy Spirit lead you. The important thing is that you start reading the Bible regularly in your alone time with Him.

On the pathway to experience God's presence, you have completed the first, and most important biblical step, of salvation. You have completed the second, and second-most-important biblical step, of spending time alone with God. You have completed the third biblical step of praying. You have completed the fourth biblical step of giving thanks. You have completed the fifth biblical step of giving praise. You have completed the sixth biblical step of worshiping. You have completed the seventh biblical step of reading the Bible. You are learning the Word of God so you can be ready for when God calls you to action. Make it a habit every day to read the Bible. Reading the Bible regularly will set you up to experience the presence of God regularly. This time must become a significant part of your life. Let God lead you and be willing to follow and obey. You may have already experienced His presence in this seventh biblical step. I encourage you to go on to the next biblical step, if the Lord leads you, because He may reveal Himself in a new way to you. Do not worry if God has not revealed Himself to you yet because it is coming. What a blessing of God!

Prayer

Dear Heavenly Father,
Please help me to have faith in Your Word, to have the desire to read Your Word, to be able to remember Your Word, to receive wisdom from Your Word, and to apply Your Word to my life. I know Your Word is powerful, and I am excited to learn it and use it to draw even closer to You. I know I cannot do anything without Your help. May all this be done for Your glory alone. I ask all of this in Jesus' name. Amen.

Declaration of Faith

God, I thank You for using the Word of God to change my life in every way for the better.

DEVOTIONAL 8

Meditate on the Bible

This book of the law shall not depart out of thy mouth;
but thou shalt meditate therein day and night, that
thou mayest observe to do according to all that is
written therein: for then thou shalt make thy way
prosperous, and then thou shalt have good success.
— Joshua 1:8

I remember working as a little boy with my mom and stepdad in the family garden. They had a huge garden, in which everything was pristine. My stepdad definitely has a green thumb, just like his dad did. I admire the talent of people who have beautiful flowers, plants, and gardens. I even enjoy going to conservatories and estates to see the perfectly manicured grounds because it is so relaxing. I have a deep appreciation for those who can make everything so beautiful because I definitely do not have any talent in these areas. I have tried to plant a purple lilac bush at our house because that is my favorite fragrance, and it has the most beautiful flowering color. Also, I have tried to plant hydrangeas because that was our wedding flower. However, everything I have ever planted never blooms and instead dies shortly after I plant it. Nothing seems to take root. Because no root is taken, there is no growth that can happen, so it just dies. Spiritually speaking, Jesus talks about how sometimes people do not have roots in the Word of God, and because of this, they fall away when difficulty comes. Meditating on the Bible will draw you even closer to God and will give you the root that you need in your walk with the Lord so you can produce fruit and accomplish His plan for your life. The Shepherd has given you, His sheep, spiritual rest through salvation, you are spending time alone with God, you are praying, you are giving thanks, you are giving praise, you are worshiping, and you are reading your Bible. Now it is time to learn the importance of meditating on the Bible, which is the eighth biblical step on the pathway to experiencing the presence of God regularly.

The reason that meditating on the Bible is the next biblical step on the pathway, after reading the Bible, is because it is time to draw even closer to God and allow the Word of God to become deeply rooted in your heart. The Word of God planting roots in your heart is what I mean by "being rooted in the Word," "being rooted in the Lord," and other similar terms. God has been preparing you as you have been reading and learning the Word of God. He is getting you ready for your call to action, but He wants you to be deeply rooted in Him before He sends you out. When you are deeply rooted in the Lord, you will not give up when you face tribulation or persecution. Also, it will help you be able to stand against the schemes of the devil (Ephesians 6:11), which will come your way as you do God's work.

A parable is an earthly story with a Heavenly meaning. Jesus showed in the Parable of the Sower (Matthew 13:1–23) that a lack of depth in the Lord is detrimental to your walk with

Him. I will summarize this parable from Matthew: The sower was a person who planted seed, and the seed was the Word of God. The sower planted the Word of God by sharing or spreading the Word of God to people. The ground into which the people received it is the ground of their hearts, and there were four types of ground: wayside, stony, thorny, and good. The seed that fell by the wayside was devoured by birds. This happens when one hears the Word and doesn't understand it, so the devil steals the Word in the person's heart. The seed that fell into stony places sprang up and was scorched by the sun, so it withered away because it had no root. This happens when one hears the Word and has joy about what was heard, but when tribulation or persecution arises because of the Word, the person gives up serving the Lord. The seed that fell among thorns was choked by the thorns. This happens when one hears the Word and then the cares of the world and the deceitfulness of riches makes it unfruitful by choking the Word in the person. The seed that fell into good ground brought forth hundredfold, sixtyfold, or thirtyfold fruit. This happens when one hears the Word, understands it, and keeps it in good ground in their heart: fruit is brought forth in the person.

Let's look closer at Matthew 13:21, which is the person who has no root of the Word of God in their heart.

> *Yet hath he not root in himself, but dureth for a while: for when tribulation or persecution ariseth because of the word, by and by he is offended.*
> — Matthew 13:21

The Greek word for "tribulation" is *thlipsis* (2347), which means tribulation, affliction, stress, pressure, or trouble. The idea is anything that causes trouble in your life. The Greek word for "persecution" is *diogmos* (1375), which means persecution, follow, or pursuit. The idea is that of being hunted. The Greek word for "offended" is *skandalizo* (4624), which means offended, cause to stumble, cause to sin, trip up, or quickly fall away. The idea is that you will stop serving the Lord. Therefore, if the Word of God is not rooted in your heart, when you face any kind of trouble that follows you, you will give up serving the Lord. This is why being rooted is so important to God because He plans on sending you out to do His work, and He does not want you to give up when it gets tough. You will face the devil and his demons, which will cause trouble in your life, and they will chase you down, trying to devour you (1 Peter 5:8). If you are not properly rooted in the Word of God, the devil and his demons will steal your soul and spirit. Reading the Bible prepares you for God's work and helps to root you by becoming spiritually minded. However, meditating on the Bible really deepens your roots and makes you even more spiritually minded. Meditating on the Bible helps to protect your mind and your entire being for the Lord.

As I mentioned earlier in this book, the devil has been trying to steal and pervert biblical words. The devil is trying to take words like *meditate* and *meditation* and give them bad meanings by putting them in his false religions. God does not want His words to be stolen by the devil. It is time that everyone understands that words like *meditate* and *meditating* are biblical words that should be used in biblical ways. Therefore, I want to teach you through the Word of God what to meditate on, how to meditate, and the benefits of meditating.

In the opening verse of this devotional message, Joshua 1:8, it says that meditating on the Bible is important. The Hebrew word for "law" in this verse is *torah* (8451), which means law, instruction, or direction. This beautifully relates to 2 Timothy 3:16, where it says that all Scripture is given for instruction. Therefore, Joshua 1:8 shows that God was talking to Joshua about all the Word of God, both Old Testament and New Testament. The idea of this part of the verse is that you are to talk about the Word of God all the time. The Hebrew word for "meditate" in this verse is *hagah* (1897), which means meditate, imagine, mutter, or ponder. The idea of this part of the verse is that you are to ponder, to think on, the Word of God by focusing on it in your mind all the time. The late great Bible teacher Derek Prince said that meditating is "learning to think God's way." The Hebrew word for "observe" in this verse is *asah* (6213), which means observe, do, make, accomplish, or become. The idea of this part of the verse is that you are to do all that is written in the Word of God by obeying. Talking about the Bible and meditating on the Bible helps you to obey the Bible. Joshua 1:8 clearly shows a progression with the Word of God that if followed and obeyed, will root your heart in the Lord. First, talk about the Word of God. Second, think on the Word of God. Third, do what the Word of God says. Notice that meditating is right in the middle, almost like the glue that holds everything together. Meditating on the Bible is essential to becoming deeply rooted in the Lord.

Now let me explain how this part of Joshua 1:8 looks on the pathway. First, the Word of God should be in your mouth, like when you are reading the Bible. You can do this by reading the Word out loud, praying the Word out loud, or declaring the Word out loud. You then take anything in the Word that really speaks to you, and you start meditating on it. What I mean by "really speaks to you" is anything that grabs your attention, anything that stands out, or anything that you want to know more about. Oftentimes, when something really speaks to you as you are reading the Bible, that is the Holy Spirit revealing to you what your focus should be, what you are to meditate on. You then meditate on what the Holy Spirit reveals to you to meditate on. You meditate by going over and over it in your mind. Yes, you may think out loud sometimes, but for the most part, it is only in your mind. You will memorize what you are meditating on because you have thought a lot about it. You are thinking about the message God is trying to convey to you through that particular passage of the Word. You are like a cow that is chewing on the cud and trying to get all the nutrients out of it. Meditating is not some complicated formula or some complicated way of thinking. It is simply taking whatever the Lord lays on your heart and mind and chewing on it. Then you will do, or become, what is written in the Word through obedience. You will be a hearer of the Word and a doer of the Word (James 1:22).

Joshua 1:8 goes on to say that if you talk, think, and act on the Word of God, you will be blessed greatly. The Hebrew word for "prosperous" in this verse is *tsalach* (6743), which means prosperous, rush, profitable, come mightily, break out, or go over. The idea of this part of the verse is that God will bless you financially. The Hebrew word for "success" in this verse is *sakal* (7919), which means success, instruction, prudence, understanding, or wisdom. The idea of this part of the verse is that God will give you what is necessary to accomplish great things. Therefore, this part of Joshua 1:8 can be summarized in this way: God will bless you greatly in every area of your life. Remember, the Bible is clear that God wants to bless you and bless others so He can be glorified (Numbers 14:21).

Numerous other Scriptures in the Bible speak of blessings that will come as a result of meditating on the Word of God. My favorites are Joshua 1:8, Psalm 1:1–6, Isaiah 26:3, and Philippians 4:8–9. You should read these Scriptures, meditate on them, memorize them, pray them, and look for the promises of God in them. If you are looking for great Scriptures on which to meditate, start with these. I have already discussed my first favorite, Joshua 1:8, so I will briefly share about the other three:

1) Psalm 1:1–6

I made mention in the fifth devotional message how fitting it is that the book of Psalms ends with six verses in Psalm 150, which is a psalm of praise. It is also fitting how the book of Psalms opens with six verses in Psalm 1, which declare how important it is to meditate on the Word of God. Psalm 1 talks about the difference between a righteous (right-doing) person and an unrighteous (wrong-doing) person. A righteous, godly person will reject the world's ways and thoughts and will replace them with God's ways and thoughts. Specifically, a righteous person meditates on the Word of God. The rewards of righteous ways and thoughts are God's blessings and Heaven. An unrighteous, ungodly person will reject God's ways and thoughts and will replace them with the world's ways and thoughts. Specifically, an unrighteous person will not meditate on the Word of God. The consequences of unrighteous ways and thoughts are curses and Hell.

Blessed is the man that walketh not in the counsel of the ungodly, nor standeth in the way of sinners, nor sitteth in the seat of the scornful.

But his delight is in the law of the LORD; and in his
     law doth he meditate day and night.
And he shall be like a tree planted by the rivers of
     water, that bringeth forth his fruit in his season;
     his leaf also shall not wither; and whatsoever he
     doeth shall prosper.
The ungodly are not so: but are like the chaff which the
     wind driveth away.
Therefore the ungodly shall not stand in the judgment,
     nor sinners in the congregation of the righteous.
For the LORD knoweth the way of the righteous: but
     the way of the ungodly shall perish.

                    — Psalm 1:1–6

2) Isaiah 26:3

Keeping your mind on God shows your faith in Him, and you will be blessed with great peace as a result.

Thou wilt keep him in perfect peace, whose mind is
stayed on thee: because he trusteth in thee.

                    — Isaiah 26:3

3) Philippians 4:8–9

God tells you specifically what to think on. The end result of obeying Him by thinking on godly things is that the God of peace will be with you. Furthermore, when someone is struggling mentally, I recommend reading and meditating on these two verses, along with all of Philippians 4.

Finally, brethren, whatsoever things are true, what-
soever things are honest, whatsoever things are
just, whatsoever things are pure, whatsoever
things are lovely, whatsoever things are of good
report; if there be any virtue, and if there be any
praise, think on these things.
Those things, which ye have both learned, and
received, and heard, and seen in me, do: and the
God of peace shall be with you.

— Philippians 4:8–9

As a television minister, interdenominational evangelist, senior pastor, and author, I love to spread the Word of God. Just like Jesus and other ministers who preach from the Bible, I am a sower who sows a large number of seeds into the hearts of people. The Lord has blessed the ministry He has given me with tremendous growth. Our television program alone goes out to millions and millions of potential viewers. Many have been saved, healed, delivered, blessed, and have experienced other miracles. As a result of doing the work of the Lord, the devil and his demons have come after my family and me in many different ways and forms. I find that Paul experienced the same thing.

I find then a law, that, when I would do good, evil is
present with me.

— Romans 7:21

Do I shudder or tremble before the demonic? *No way!* I know the Holy Spirit inside of me is greater than the devil or any demon (1 John 4:4). God has taught me how to defeat the demonic through a three-step process: Accept, Build, and Command. I like to refer to this process as *Defeating Demons*. I will share with you the highlights of what I do in this process so you can also do the same and defeat demons.

Defeating Demons

1. *Accept* — I have repented, confessed, and accepted Jesus Christ as my Lord and personal Savior (Matthew 4:17; Romans 10:9-13).
2. *Build* — I continue to build a deeper relationship, fellowship, and friendship with Jesus by giving myself fully to Him and submitting myself fully to Him (Romans 12:1–2; James 4:7).
3. *Command* — I use the Word of God to resist the demonic, and I bind, rebuke, and command every demon that may be behind anyone or anything to leave in the name of Jesus (Matthew 4; James 4:7; Matthew 18:18; Luke 4:35; Jude 9).

Demons can possess (live inside) the non-Christian (Mark 5:1-20). Demons *cannot* possess the Christian (Romans 8:9-11; 1 Corinthians 3:16-17; 1 John 5:18). However, demons can oppress (overpower; treat harshly) various areas in the life of the non-Christian and the Christian (Acts 10:38). Non-Christians and Christians can use the process of *Defeating Demons* to defeat the demonic in every way and in every area. God gave me this revelation and many other revelations as I have spent time alone with Him reading, meditating, and obeying His Word. I learned many years ago the importance of reading and obeying His Word. I have since learned the importance and necessity of meditating on the Word. Meditating on the Word has deepened my walk in the Lord and has brought me wonderful peace. Furthermore, as a result of reading, meditating, and obeying the Bible, I have the power of God, and He has greatly blessed me. I am firmly rooted in Him and sealed by the Holy Spirit. I will forever serve God, knowing that I have given myself to Him and that He will keep me (2 Timothy 1:12).

Do you meditate on the Bible regularly? I hope this devotional message spoke to your heart and mind and gave you the desire to do so. You need to meditate on the Bible as part of the pathway. God loves to have you experience His presence by giving you revelations of His Word when you meditate on His Bible. You can pray for God to help you meditate on the Bible, and He will. You are the receiver of the seed, so you must determine what you are going to do with what you receive. Therefore, make sure your heart is good ground and ready to receive the Word. Then meditate on the Word, which will deepen your roots in the Lord. Remember, the biblical steps are not difficult and are not meant to be, which is why I spend a lot of time focusing on the importance of the biblical step. However, now is the time to take the knowledge I have shared with you and start meditating every day. Meditating can take biblical knowledge and turn it into spiritual meat. You will receive the peace of God, the power of God, and the blessings of God. You will become firmly rooted in Him, never to be plucked away by the demonic. Let the Spirit of God lead you in every way in the area of meditating.

On the pathway to experience God's presence, you have completed the first, and most important biblical step, of salvation. You have completed the second, and second-most-important biblical step, of spending time alone with God. You have completed the third biblical step of praying. You have completed the fourth biblical step of giving thanks. You have completed the fifth biblical step of giving praise. You have completed the sixth biblical step of worshiping. You have completed the seventh biblical step of reading the Bible. You have completed the eighth biblical step of meditating on the Bible. You are becoming deeply and firmly rooted in the Lord. Make it a habit every day to meditate on the Bible. Meditating on the Bible regularly will set you up to experience the presence of God regularly. This time must become a significant part of your life. Let God lead you and be willing to follow and obey. You may have already experienced His presence in this eighth biblical step. I encourage you to go on to the next biblical step, if the Lord leads you, because He may reveal Himself in a new way to you. Do not worry if God has not revealed Himself to you yet because it is coming. What a blessing of God!

Prayer

Dear Heavenly Father,

Please help me to meditate on Your Word. I want to be deeply and firmly rooted in You and be spiritually minded. Protect my family and me always from the demonic and help us to defeat the demonic through the name of Jesus. Please bless us greatly with all Your blessings. May all this be done for Your glory alone. I ask all of this in Jesus' name. Amen.

Declaration of Faith

God, I thank You for deeply and firmly rooting me in You through meditating on Your holy and glorious Word.

DEVOTIONAL 9

Wait on God

Wait on the LORD, and keep his way, and he shall exalt thee to inherit the land: when the wicked are cut off, thou shalt see it.

— Psalm 37:34

Everyone has an area of life in which they struggle and are vulnerable for attack by the devil and his demons. Some struggle with various addictions, depression, anxiety, gluttony, swearing, pornography, lying, envy, coveting, sickness, illness, and disease, to name just a few. There are countless areas in which people struggle. Oftentimes, numerous demons are behind those areas. Thankfully, since Jesus Christ overcame the world, through His power you can have peace and overcome every area in which you struggle (John 16:33).

I used to struggle with worry, but God set me free. If worry tries to come against me now, I use the process of *Defeating Demons*. The worry is gone immediately, because it works every time in every area where the demonic is present.

If you are sick in any way, sometimes it is caused by or linked with the demonic. If the demonic is behind it, defeat the demon(s), then believe and claim your healing by the stripes of Jesus, and you will be healed (Isaiah 53:5; 1 Peter 2:24). Your sickness may not be directly a result of or associated with the demonic. It may be because of your sin. Be quick to repent and confess your sin by asking God to forgive you in the name of Jesus, and He will forgive you. Then believe and claim your healing by the stripes of Jesus, and you will be healed.

Your sickness may not be directly a result of your sin. It may be because you, and everyone on earth, lives in a fallen world and the world is in a fallen state. You can still believe and claim your healing by the stripes of Jesus, and you will be healed. I used to struggle with being sick a lot, but now I walk in divine health, and you can, too. The Word of God is quick and powerful (Hebrews 4:12). Therefore, apply the Word of God to your situation, and God will work everything out because He is faithful that promised (Hebrews 10:23).

At times I still struggle with being patient. I am not good at waiting in general. God has been working with me in this area of my life, and I can see major progress. I am not yet where I need to be, but I know I will get there with the Lord's help.

The Shepherd has given you, His sheep, spiritual rest through salvation, you are spending time alone with God, you are praying, you are giving thanks, you are giving praise, you are worshiping, you are reading your Bible, and you are meditating on the Bible. Now it is time to learn the importance of waiting on God, which is the ninth and final and third-most-important biblical step on the pathway to experiencing His presence regularly.

The reason that waiting on God is the ninth and final and third-most-important biblical step on the pathway, after meditating on the Bible, is because you have been seeking God on the pathway, but now God is ready to come seek after you. Waiting on God is the final biblical step of seeking God on the pathway, and waiting on Him will cause Him to come to you.

He seeks after you because He wants to bless you with experiencing His presence. Maybe you have or have not experienced His presence in previous biblical steps. However, this final biblical step is where I have found that God reveals Himself the most. This is where God comes looking for you. Of course, you must be saved, which is the first-most-important biblical step because without salvation you cannot experience all that God has for you. You must spend time alone with God, which is the second-most-important biblical step because once you are alone with Him the atmosphere is set up the way He wants it to be so you can meet with Him. You are starting the process for the special meeting that will take place between you and Him. You must wait on God, which is the third-most-important biblical step because waiting on Him sets everything up for Him to come to you. He will be coming with His great blessings. He will be coming to reveal Himself to you. It is time to experience God's presence in whatever way He chooses to manifest Himself to you.

Remember, God can reveal His presence to you in a limitless number of ways. I will share with you again some of the ways that I have experienced God's presence, combined with ways the Bible describes. Again, this is not a complete list because there are a host of ways that God may reveal His presence to you. God may reveal His presence to you by pressing something on your heart and mind by giving you a promise, godly thought, idea, or answer to a problem or situation. He may make the Word of God come alive so that it really speaks to you when you are reading it, studying it, or meditating on it. You may hear an audible voice, have a vision, or have a godly dream. He may heal your body or give your body rest. He may answer one or several of your prayers. He may send someone to speak a word from God to you. He may open or close a door of opportunity. The presence of God may cause you to experience the fruit of the Spirit, be still, be in awe of Him, be silent, or even cry. He may manifest His presence to you by causing you to physically feel or see a display of His power.

Again, it is worth repeating that the number-one way God has manifested His presence to me during my alone times with Him is by pressing something on my heart and mind through His still, small voice, which many times leaves me in awe of Him. This pressing has happened to me oftentimes in the form of a promise, godly thought, idea, or answer to a problem or situation. When this pressing happens, I know beyond a shadow of a doubt that it is God speaking to me. I do not have to question or wonder because I know His voice. I know His voice because I have spent time with Him, I have a relationship with Him, and He makes His voice clear. I experience God's presence in the greatest degree during my waiting time on the pathway. As a result, the relationship, fellowship, and friendship I have with Him grows and grows. God speaks and my faith grows, it is a beautiful thing.

God wants to speak to your heart and mind in a powerful way. He wants to give you direction, encouragement, and build your faith. You will notice that the word He speaks to you will cause a tremendous and noticeable increase in your faith. This perfectly matches what the Bible says.

> *So then faith cometh by hearing, and hearing by the word of God.*
> — Romans 10:17

The Greek word for "word" is *rhema* (4487), which means word, a thing spoken, utterance, or promise. This verse shows that when you hear a word spoken from the Lord, faith will come. Therefore, God can speak a word to you as you read and meditate on the Bible as a way to increase your faith. God also can speak a direct word to you anytime He chooses, which will cause your faith to grow. This is experiencing the presence of God. You wait, He speaks, and your faith grows.

Many times, you may think you are waiting on God, but He is actually waiting on you because He wants to be gracious to you. He is waiting for you to meet His terms and conditions. He is waiting for you to give yourself completely to Him. He is waiting for you to wait on Him. As you wait on Him, He will seek you and show up with His blessings.

> *And therefore will the LORD wait, that he may be gracious unto you, and therefore will he be exalted, that he may have mercy upon you: for the LORD is a God of judgment: blessed are all they that wait for him.*
>
> — Isaiah 30:18

So, what exactly does it mean to wait on God? In the opening verse of this devotional message, Psalm 37:34, it says that you need to "wait on the Lord." The Hebrew word for "wait" is *qavah* (6960), which means wait, wait for, look, or expect. The idea of this part of the verse is that you are staying where you are, looking for God, because you are expecting God to come through in a glorious way. In other words, waiting on God is focusing your total attention on looking for Him to show up anytime. Looking expectantly shows that even while you are waiting, you have faith, and it is in action. You are expecting God to arrive anytime and speak to you, answer your prayer, bless you, or do something else great. You now understand that waiting involves expectancy, which is your faith in action as you wait. Think of expectancy as the umbrella of the biblical step of waiting on God. Like an umbrella, expectancy is over everything you do in this biblical step. In other words, everything in this biblical step involves expectancy. Again, expectancy is your faith in action as you wait. God has revealed to me what to specifically do while I wait on God with expectancy, and now I will share it with you.

Under the umbrella of expectancy, there are three things you are to do that will help you to properly wait on the Lord: Be silent, be still, and be patient.

1) BE SILENT

You may have been talking out loud as you have been praying, giving thanks, giving praise, worshiping, reading your Bible, and meditating on the Bible. Do not get me wrong, your talking has been good and necessary. You have glorified God. However, now it is time to *not* talk, which will also glorify God.

> *Be silent, O all flesh, before the* Lord: *for he is raised up out of his holy habitation.*
>
> — Zechariah 2:13

The Hebrew word for "silent" is *has* (2013), which means silent, still, keep silence, or hold tongue. The idea of this part of the verse is not to audibly talk. Therefore, you are to be silent by not saying a word. It is time to get ready for God to speak. Stay expectant as you are silently waiting. Maybe you have been thinking as you have read this section that you have done everything along the pathway in your mind, without speaking out loud. No worries, because the second thing you are to do while you wait covers the mind.

2) BE STILL

You may have been praying with your hands folded, raising your hands giving God thanks and praise, bowing before God in worship, or turning the pages of your Bible as you read and meditated on the Word. Do not get me wrong, your movements have been good and necessary. You have glorified God. However, now it is time to *not* move, which will also glorify God.

> *Be still, and know that I am God: I will be exalted*
> *among the heathen, I will be exalted in the earth.*
> — Psalm 46:10

The Hebrew word for "still" is *raphah* (7503), which means still, relax, faint, cease, or sink. The idea of this part of the verse is to stop moving. In addition, the definition means to relax. Relaxing is something you must do physically and mentally. You relax the body and the mind. Therefore, you are to be still by not moving and not thinking. Give your body and mind a break. It is God's turn for action, and He will fill your mind with what He wants. Stay expectant as you are waiting in stillness both physically and mentally.

3) BE PATIENT

You have been seeking Him and wanting to have a glorious spiritual experience. Do not get me wrong, your search for Him and your desire to experience His presence have been godly. You have glorified God. However, now it is time to be patient, which will also glorify God.

> *Rest in the LORD, and wait patiently for him: fret not thyself because of him who prospereth in his way, because of the man who bringeth wicked devices to pass.*
>
> — Psalm 37:7

The Hebrew word for "rest" is *damam* (1826), which means rest, silent, still, stop, wait, or quiet self. The idea of this part of the verse shows that resting in the Lord means to wait. Resting is how you are to wait. Resting involves being silent and being still, both physically and mentally. This reiterates what I have already taught you so far. The Hebrew word for "patiently" is *chuwl* (2342), which means patiently, bear, writhe, bring forth, pain, or trust. The idea of this part of the verse is that you are to trust in God. At times it may be painful to trustingly wait, but God will come through by bringing forth something great. That is why this verse opens by telling you to rest. You are to be totally dependent, physically and mentally, on the power and strength of the Holy Spirit. He will strengthen you and calm you. God is not rushed. He will speak and move when He is ready. Therefore, be patient by letting God be in total control of you. It is God's turn to come to you with His blessings in His timing, so stay expectant as you wait patiently.

You have waited, and now God comes with His blessings. He comes with His blessings of graciousness, mercy, and happiness (Isaiah 30:18). He comes with His blessings of inheritance and seeing the wicked cut off (Psalm 37:34). He also comes with His blessing of having you experience His presence in one way or in multiple ways. As I have shown you through-out this book, there are countless ways to experience His presence, and they are all a blessing from the Lord. Your Heavenly Father coming to you, as you are waiting on Him, brings the greatest blessing you could ever have: God Himself. Having a deeper relationship, fellowship, and friendship with God is the best thing ever because you are getting to know the greatest Person ever, God Eternal. In the Bible, God revealed this truth to Abraham, and now He is revealing this truth to you.

> *After these things the word of the LORD came unto Abram in a vision, saying, Fear not, Abram: I am thy shield, and thy exceeding great reward.*
> — Genesis 15:1

I told you at the beginning of this devotional message that I often struggle with being patient, but I am getting better with the Lord's help. I now practice the biblical step of waiting on God every time I go through the pathway. I wait with expectancy. I take the time to be silent, still, and patient. I stop speaking, stop moving, clear all thoughts out of my mind, and become in no hurry. Waiting for me at first was hard because I was not used to being quiet, holding still, keeping my mind free from thoughts, and taking my time. However, the more I have practiced all of this, the better I have gotten. I now enjoy waiting on God so much that it is one of my favorite biblical steps to practice after salvation and being alone with God. Sometimes I will take thirty minutes or longer just to wait. Even if I only have an hour to spend seeking the Lord, sometimes half of my time is spent waiting on God. Only God could take someone like me, who has been impatient most of my life, and change me so that waiting on Him is one of my favorite things. I find that waiting on God is a restful experience, just like Psalm 37:7 says.

Many times, as I begin the waiting phase, God will speak to my heart and mind, telling me that He is with me. It is as if God is letting me know that as I begin waiting on Him, He is there, even though I might not have sensed Him in any other way. It is like when I go into my kids' rooms at night as they began to lie down, and I tell them that I love them. It is a reassurance for them that I am there for them and love them. This helps my kids to sleep peacefully. I have fallen asleep many times during this time of waiting on the Lord because it is so restful and peaceful, knowing my Father is there. However, most of the time I stay awake while I wait on God, and He manifests His presence to me. Oftentimes I experience His presence by Him pressing something on my heart and mind through His still, small voice, which many times leaves me in awe of Him. Many times, His still, small voice gives me a promise, a godly thought, an idea, or an answer to a problem or situation. If I had been talking, moving, thinking, or being impatient, I would not have heard His voice. Elijah also experienced God's presence through a still, small voice when he was alone with Him (1 Kings 19).

Do you wait on God regularly? I hope this devotional message spoke to your heart and mind and gave you the desire to do so. You need to wait on God. God may lead you to wait on Him, at the start of every biblical step on the pathway, so you know exactly what to do in that biblical step. However, waiting on God needs to also be practiced as its own biblical step. He loves to have you experience His presence by speaking to your heart and mind as you wait on Him. You can pray for

God to help you wait on Him, and He will. Waiting on God may seem hard at first, but it will quickly become one of your favorite and most powerful biblical steps. The rest and peace you will experience is divine. God will seek you as you wait on Him, and He will bring His many blessings to you. The greatest blessing you will receive is God Himself. Let the Spirit of God lead you in every way in the area of waiting on Him.

On the pathway to experience God's presence, you have completed the first, and most important biblical step, of salvation. You have completed the second, and second-most-important biblical step, of spending time alone with God. You have completed the third biblical step of praying. You have completed the fourth biblical step of giving thanks. You have completed the fifth biblical step of giving praise. You have completed the sixth biblical step of worshiping. You have completed the seventh biblical step of reading the Bible. You have completed the eighth biblical step of meditating on the Bible. You have completed the ninth and final, and third-most-important biblical step, of waiting on God. Your Heavenly Father has sought you and brought you the greatest blessing, Himself. You are becoming rooted even deeper in the Lord. Make it a habit every day to wait on the Lord. Waiting on God regularly will set you up to experience His presence regularly. This time must become a significant part of your life. Let God lead you and be willing to follow and obey. You may have already experienced His presence in this ninth biblical step. If you feel led to go back to a previous biblical step, then do so because He may reveal Himself in a new way to you. Do not worry if God has not revealed Himself to you yet because it is coming. If you are done for the day seeking the Lord using the pathway, do it again tomorrow. Your process may vary when it comes to what biblical steps you do and in what order you do them to experience God's presence. Just remember, it all starts and ends with Jesus. Let the Holy Spirit lead you.

Even if you are not able to be alone, you can still seek God anywhere, anytime, and with anyone around. You can always make sure you are right with God, pray, give thanks, praise, worship, read the Bible, meditate on the Bible, and wait on God (1 Thessalonians 5). The more you grow in the Lord, the more you will do all these things without ceasing. I enjoy doing all these things as much as I can. However, it is such a blessed and powerful experience to do all these things while you are alone with God.

God has been specifically teaching me and speaking to me about waiting on Him all the time, even when I am not alone with Him on the pathway. Sometimes waiting is short-term and sometimes it is long-term. It is up to God. Waiting helps me put God first, acknowledge Him as my Source, humble myself, and build my relationship, fellowship, and friendship with Him. I love to wait on God all the time.

> *Lead me in thy truth, and teach me: for thou art the*
> *God of my salvation; on thee do I wait all the day.*
> — Psalm 25:5

A Christian friend of mine, Billy Robinson, recently said he was praying for me and that God had showed him something in the spiritual realm. He saw a rainbow with a gift tag on it, and he saw me in the background inside a big church. He knew God was showing him that He had a promise for me. After Billy told me that, I went home, got alone, and prayed to God about this. The Lord spoke to me that He was ready to answer all the things I had been praying about. Furthermore, God said that I needed to start looking for the answers, just like one looks for a rainbow after the rain when the sun is shining. I understood exactly what God was telling me in my spirit. God was telling me to wait all day on Him while looking with expectancy for His answers to my prayers that are on the way. As a confirmation from God, just a few weeks prior, I had taken a photo outside of a double rainbow. I received all this in Jesus' holy name. The good news is that He will do the same for you. Start waiting all day while releasing your faith by looking for His blessings that are coming quickly. What a blessing of God!

I love you, and God bless you. Please pray for my family, me, and my ministry, and we will do the same for you.

Prayer

Dear Heavenly Father,
Please help me to wait on You with silence, stillness, and patience. Please come to me and let me discover the exceeding great reward that is You. May all this be done for Your glory alone. I ask all of this in Jesus' name. Amen.

Declaration of Faith

God, I thank You for helping me to wait on You.

HOW THE LORD BECAME MY SHEPHERD

From the Beginning

*For I know the thoughts that I think toward you,
saith the LORD, thoughts of peace, and not of evil, to
give you an expected end.*
— Jeremiah 29:11

My mother, Ellen, noticed I had a calling on my life before I was born. She remembers that I constantly moved in her belly during church services as though I were praising the Lord. When I was around the age of two, my parents and I had a direct encounter with an angel from God and a demon. It happened when my mother was abruptly awoken out of her sleep and saw me standing at the entrance of their bedroom. I was rubbing my eyes, and she told me to come and get in bed. However, she unexpectedly noticed an angelic being standing behind me waving his hands. The angelic being was a male angel, and there was a bright light shining around him. He was translucent, wearing a long white robe with wide sleeves. Suddenly my mother noticed that it was not me standing there, but that it was my spirit. She woke up my father, but he did not see anything.

My mother started praying that I would come and get in bed with them if I was going to live. She prayed hard until she somehow fell back asleep. Without warning, she was awakened to me crawling in bed with them. The angel then appeared to her in the same spot again. She woke up my father again, but he still did not see the angel. Then I said, "Mommy, I see... I see... a man in white," which surprised my parents because that was before I could even speak full sentences and before I knew my colors. My parents were amazed, and somehow, everyone fell asleep.

My father then dreamed that an angel touched the bed, and it began to spin. My father woke everyone up, and this time, my mother saw a man dressed in all black, with red eyes, and his skin looked like charcoal. He was clearly a demonic being. He stared at all three of us and then walked out of the trailer through the wall. My father did not see him, but he believed what my mother saw. My mother believed that this series of events meant that God had something special planned for me, but the devil was angry and wanted to stop it. It was shortly after that incident that my parents went through a divorce, no doubt an attack of the devil.

Both of my parents would later remarry other people when I was about eight. I went to church with my mother and stepfather, and with my father and stepmother when they went. I can recall most of those times. I can remember seeing the people, hearing the music, and listening to the preachers. I can even remember giggling at some of the strange and vibrant-colored suits some of the men wore that were popular at the time. The main thing I recall was how nice everyone was to me.

God Uses My Grandparents

As I got older, I started to spend more time with my paternal grandparents, Robert and Lena Branham. They were both originally from eastern Kentucky, and they both moved to northern Ohio when they were young. They were both raised in the ways of God. They met and married at a young age. They loved God, Jesus, and the Holy Spirit. They loved going to church. I started going to church with them every opportunity I could because they exuded the love of God, and it drew me to them.

I went to church with my grandparents two to three times a week. They would get there early to open the church doors, to turn on the lights, and to make sure everything was just perfect and ready to go. My wonderful Sunday school teachers taught me the Ten Commandments, the Twelve Beatitudes, how Jesus loved me, and how enjoyable it is to serve God. I even participated in church plays, which was definitely not my strong suit. At some of the services, I would take a nap in my pew. Church provided for some of the best napping because it was the most peaceful place a kid could be. However, most of the time, I was a giant sponge soaking in everything I could about God. I began to understand what it meant to have a relationship with God.

My grandparents were a wonderful example of a happily married couple who put God first in every way. They were hard workers, kind, and selfless. I watched them, and I wanted to be like them when I grew up. They were a strong-in-the-faith family that loved the Lord. They let their light shine, just like Christ taught in the Gospels. I saw their good works, and so did others. They did not boast about their good works but rather just performed them in a loving way, which brought glory to God.

> *Let your light so shine before men, that they may see your good works, and glorify your Father which is in heaven.*
>
> — Matthew 5:16

God Speaks to Me Directly

In 1998 when I was fifteen, I began to slowly drift away from God. One night, when I was on my way back home after hanging out with friends, I felt something tell me to put on my seat belt. Before I knew it, I was in a bad car accident. I asked the EMT if I was going to live as I was being rushed to the hospital. The EMT plainly said, "I don't know." I was bleeding profusely from a face trauma. The hospital did a CT scan of my head, and then I was put in a dark, quiet room while they called my family in.

As I lay in that hospital room, I noticed that God was speaking to me. It was not an audible voice, but a still, small voice that was pressing on my heart and mind. It was hard to explain, but I knew it was God. God was knocking on the door of my heart, and He wanted me to let Him in all the way.

> *Behold, I stand at the door, and knock: if any man hear my voice, and open the door, I will come in to him, and will sup with him, and he with me.*
>
> — Revelation 3:20

God started speaking to me, telling me that if I would have died, I would have gone to Hell because I had turned my back on Him. That may sound like God was being harsh, but He was not. God told me in such a loving way that it caused me to want to change and be fully committed to Him like never before. I told God that if He would spare me, I would serve Him all the days of my life. In the stillness of that hospital room, all alone, I repented, confessed, and accepted Jesus Christ as my Lord and personal Savior.

The doctor came back into the room to further examine me. The doctor said I could have died instantly based on the way my face struck the car on impact. He said I would need to see a plastic surgeon for reconstructive surgery on my nose and face. The doctor called my survival a miracle. I knew it was an act of God that I was alive. God spared me, saved me, and finished His healing work in me. My body healed in such a great way that I have never had to have any kind of reconstructive surgery.

Called to Preach

After my car accident, I started going to church again like never before. I went with my grandparents, with friends, with anyone else who would go, and by myself. I tried my best to be there whenever the doors were open. On April 7, 1999, at the age of sixteen, during a Wednesday night youth church service, I felt God speak to me directly again. God pressed on my heart and mind that I was called to preach. I knew it was God speaking to me again.

I hurried home that night to tell my mother the good news. She gave me the advice not to tell anyone but to wait and see if

God really was calling me to minister. Shortly after that, evangelist and senior pastor Rev. Ralph Farmer asked me when I was going to preach for him at his church. That same day, a musician named R. B. Fallen asked me when I was going to preach. I asked R. B. how he knew that I was called to preach. R. B. smiled and said, "I can just tell." I knew that God used Rev. Ralph Farmer and R. B. Fallen to confirm my calling.

On May 14, 1999, at Rev. Ralph Farmer's church in North Fairfield, Ohio, I preached my first sermon to a packed country church with 105 people in attendance. The sermon was titled "Trust." It lasted twelve minutes. One person repented, confessed, and accepted Jesus Christ as their Lord and personal Savior. It was evident to everyone in attendance that I was truly called by God to preach. From that point on, ministers from all denominations began to contact me about preaching at their churches. Rev. Ken Gifford, a local minister, took me under his wing and helped to mentor me in a variety of areas regarding ministry. I continued to minister and grow in the faith, and I soon began my Christian studies. I was ordained in 2003, at the age of twenty, by Ripley Chapel, a nondenominational church. I became an interdenominational evangelist, filling in for all denominations, spreading the Good News of Jesus Christ.

God Blesses Me with a Wife

In 2004, at the age of twenty-one, I graduated from North Central State College (NCSC) as a registered nurse (RN) to help supplement my income. In the fall, I started praying that God would send me the wife He had prepared for me. I read Christian books about love and prayed a lot on this topic. God was putting this desire in me for a reason. I had peace that God would send me a wife in His perfect timing.

Later in 2004, I started seeing this beautiful woman around town. She had a contagious smile, dark brown hair, and dark brown eyes. I saw her at the hospital while I took care of her father, I saw her at the tire shop of all places, and I saw her in other places around our local community. I knew exactly who she was. Her name was Victoria, and she had been a senior in high school when I was a freshman. I remember thinking in high school how beautiful she was. However, I was a freshman, so I did not even try talking with her. Also, I had worked with her before, in 2002, at Pepperidge Farm, on one of the packaging lines while we were on summer break from college. The funny thing is, I had worked right beside her, and we did not even talk. She was not a Christian when we worked together, so it was not God's timing yet for us to get to know each other. God was preparing her first to become a Christian, and she did. By the time I started seeing her around town a lot, she had become a committed follower of Jesus Christ. I would later find out that she became a Christian when she heard television minister Dr. Creflo Dollar give an altar call. She got on her knees in her apartment, and right there on the spot, she repented, confessed, and accepted Jesus Christ as her Lord and personal Savior. It changed her life. She started going to church and growing greatly in the faith.

I made up my mind that the next time I saw her, I was going to ask her out. As God would have it, on December 20, 2004, I got my chance. I had gone to Cleveland, Ohio, with my friend Ryan, and I was supposed to be back in town for a family event by 6:00 p.m. However, the roads were not good, and there was no way I was going to get back in time. As I got closer to home, Ryan asked if we could stop at Barnes & Noble so he could purchase a book. I agreed because I knew I was not going to be able to make it to my family event on time. Almost as soon as I walked through the doors at Barnes & Noble, I saw Victoria there in the store. God quickly reminded me that I had promised myself to ask her out the next time I saw her. God was not going to let me forget or chicken out. I mustered up the confidence and asked her if she would like to go out sometime. I thought in my head there was no chance she would say yes, but I had to at least ask. She smiled and said she would. I could not believe it. We stayed and talked for over an hour at the store until she had to leave to get ready for work because she now worked third shift full-time at Pepperidge Farm. Ryan and I left Barnes & Noble and stopped at another store and then stopped to get gas. There Victoria was at the gas station. Victoria and I laughed, smiled, and waved. Four days later, on December 24, 2004, Victoria and I had our first official date at a Christmas Eve church service. We were married on August 11, 2007, with Rev. Ken Gifford performing the ceremony.

Pastoring and Family

Victoria and I went all over evangelizing. I regularly preached at Ripley Chapel, which was the first church to license and ordain me. They asked me if I would fill in for them long-term until they found a pastor. In January 2008, I started to fill in for them with the understanding that they would not call me "pastor." I did not want to be called a pastor because I viewed myself only as an interdenominational evangelist. However, Ronnie Horsley, the head of the church board, introduced me to the congregation by calling me "pastor." I continue to be their senior pastor to this day while still evangelizing inter-denominationally. God has taught me so much about His character and how to be a servant since I have been a senior pastor. Furthermore, our church has supported our evangelistic ministry faithfully.

In 2009, Victoria and I were blessed with our first son, Ricky. In 2011, we were blessed with another son, Riley. In 2013, we were blessed with a daughter, Vera. God expanded our family and provided the perfect church setting for us to raise our children in the Lord. Our children continue to serve the Lord both in the church setting and in the evangelistic setting. We look forward to seeing God continue to use them in great ways for His glory.

Education

I continued my education by enrolling in the School of Ministry and the Church of God's ministerial programs. I received the Church of God's licensure and ordination as a minister. I also completed my bachelor of arts (BA) degree in organizational management and my master of business administration (MBA) degree from Malone University. Victoria completed her master of business administration (MBA) degree from Malone University as well. She also completed business certifications through the Harvard School of Business.

Television, Radio, and Social Media

I have always had the desire to be a television minister, ever since God called me to preach. The fourth message I ever preached, on July 6, 1999, was on television because I was an invited guest by Rev. Ralph Farmer. It was on WGGN-TV 52 in northern Ohio. That would be the only time I would preach on television until over twenty years later. I had stopped seeking God about becoming a television minister because I did not see it as something that was going to happen. However, God, in His infinite wisdom, mercy, and grace, did not forget about the dream He had placed in my heart so long ago.

God had prepared blessings for me and millions of people around the world using television, radio, and social media. It all began in March 2020, when I started diligently seeking God's face and His ways like never before while alone in my prayer closet, also known as my bedroom. Diligently seeking God means to well and thoroughly desire to know Him and His ways by spending time with Him. As a result, I started experiencing the presence of God regularly. During one of these times in my prayer closet, God pressed on my heart and mind to begin a Facebook ministry because many churches were closed due to the COVID-19 pandemic. I was rather reluctant to begin this type of ministry, but I followed His leading and obeyed.

On September 30, 2020, I met with a preacher who was on television who had seen my Facebook sermons. He told me he liked how biblically based they were. The preacher asked me if I had ever thought about television ministry. He did not know that when I was sixteen and first started preaching, I wanted to be a television minister. When he asked me that question, something came alive in me and stirred again my desire to preach on television. However, I did not know how I could preach on television, considering I lived in a small community and pastored a small church. I went to the Lord and prayed about it in my prayer closet. I experienced the presence of the Lord, and He pressed on my heart and mind what to do next.

The Lord led me to the next step of contacting WGGN-TV 52, which I did. On October 21, 2020, exactly three weeks from when I was asked if I had ever thought about television ministry, I had a television contract with WGGN-TV 52 and was taping in their studio. My television program, *Ricky Branham Ministries*, first aired on November 25, 2020, at 6 p.m., on WGGN-TV 52 in Ohio. The title of my first television sermon was "Remember Your Testimonies." My first radio program aired on WLRD 96.9 FM in Ohio on November 29, 2020. On February 2, 2021, my television program aired for the first time on WLLA-TV 64 in Michigan. On June 5, 2021, my television program first aired nationally through the GEB Television Network, which is owned and operated by Oral Roberts University.

My television program has since expanded to many more networks in the United States, and it continues to grow nationally and internationally. It airs in all fifty states and reaches a potential audience of over seventy-eight million people a week and growing. Search on your television for your local TV listing: *Ricky Branham Ministries*. God has amazed me with how He has wonderfully orchestrated everything regarding this television ministry. He has given me a great Christian agent, the perfect church for production, an amazingly talented producer, a quality closed-captioning company to work with, and the list goes on. The television networks have been an absolute pleasure to work with as we work together to spread God's Word. All this has been wonderfully orchestrated by God for this small-town preacher. God has done it in such a way that only

He can receive the glory. God's blessings have literally chased me down!

I regularly seek the Lord to know His will in the areas of television, radio, and social media. He continues to reveal Himself to me to show me His will. I follow and obey His leading. As a result, I have experienced great blessings and many miracles, and so have others. I have been blessed to see many people around the world repent, confess, and accept Jesus Christ as their Lord and personal Savior. God is being glorified all over the world. My prayer is that I would see one million people come to know Jesus Christ as their Lord and personal Savior from the ministry He has gifted me with.

Master of Theology (ThM), Doctor of Ministry (DMIN), and Author

I had thought I was done with college, at least from the standpoint of pursuing degrees. I had originally wanted to obtain my doctorate, but then I thought maybe it was not meant to be, so I had given up on the idea. However, God clearly showed me He wanted me to go to college for my doctorate, and He opened the door for me to do so. I also knew it was God when the president of the college said I could write a book as my doctoral dissertation. God had already birthed in me an idea for a book, but I had no clue how it could ever come to fruition. God showed me by opening the door for me to write a book while earning my doctorate degree.

The book I wrote while working on my doctorate in college was *Psalm 23: A Psalm for the Living*. I graduated from the Christian Bible Institute and Seminary (CBIS) with a master of theology (ThM) degree and a doctor of ministry (DMin) degree in April 2022. After graduation, I submitted my book to a select group of publishers. An executive from Trilogy Publishing, a subsidiary of the Trinity Broadcast Network (TBN), reached out to me and said that he liked how I used so many Bible references in my book. He said he believes the more Scriptures an author uses, the less error there is. He and his team did a full review of my book and offered me a contract, which I accepted. *WOW! Glory to God!* I knew all this was of God because He had already told me that my main calling and avenue of ministry would be through television. Therefore, it made sense that God would use a Christian television network to publish my book. Furthermore, I had grown up watching TBN, and I am beyond honored to be a part of their family.

I noticed a theme with God: God does the impossible. He is a Doctor who specializes in the impossible. I had a dream to become a television minister when I was first called to preach, but I had given up on that. It seemed impossible. I had a desire to obtain my doctorate, but I had given up on that. It seemed impossible. I wanted to write a book and have it published, but I did not see how that could ever happen. It seemed impossible. God has made everything happen in His time. God does the impossible. He is a Doctor who specializes in the impossible!

Going Forward

I continue to minister all over, spreading the Good News of Jesus Christ as a television minister, interdenominational evangelist, senior pastor, and author. *Ricky Branham Ministries* (RBM) desires to reach the lost, edify the saints, and minister to people of all ages and in all walks of life for the glory of Jesus

Christ. God can do the impossible, and God desires to do the impossible.

> *But Jesus beheld them, and said unto them, With men this is impossible; but with God all things are possible.*
> — Matthew 19:26

My television program, *Ricky Branham Ministries*, has expanded to many more networks in the United States, and it continues to grow nationally and internationally. It airs in all fifty states and reaches a potential audience of over seventy-eight million people a week and growing. Search on your television for your local TV listing: *Ricky Branham Ministries*. I also frequently appear as a guest on many Christian television programs throughout the United States. On my social media pages, I post a lot of ministry content, so please follow, like, and share. Search: *Ricky Branham Ministries* on Facebook, YouTube, and Instagram.

As an interdenominational evangelist, I travel all over and preach at all churches and ministry events that proclaim Jesus Christ as Lord and personal Savior. I am the senior pastor of a nondenominational church, Ripley Chapel. I continue to serve and preach at my home church when I am not traveling. As an author, I hope that my books teach and inspire you to grow closer to God, to live in victory, and to see the impossible happen. I pray that I leave everyone with a message from God that is timely, memorable, and applicable. If you would like to have me speak at your church or ministry event, please contact *Ricky Branham Ministries* through my website: www.rickybranham.com or through my social media platforms.

REFERENCES

Bible Hub online. https://biblehub.com/.

Strong, James. *The New Strong's Exhaustive Concordance of the Bible: with main concordance, appendix to the main concordance, topical index to the Bible, dictionary of the Hebrew Bible, dictionary of the Greek Testament.* Nashville: Thomas Nelson Publishers, 1996.

OTHER WORKS BY
DR. RICKY BRANHAM

PSALM 23: A PSALM FOR THE LIVING

23 Devotional Messages to Lead You to the Blessings of Salvation, Overflow, and Eternal Life

DR. RICKY BRANHAM

"READINGS FOR YOUR PRAYER CLOSET"
DEVOTIONAL MESSAGE SERIES — BOOK 1

Do you need a miracle spiritually, physically, mentally, emotionally, relationally, or financially?

God has your miracle and wants to deliver it to you quickly. Your answer can be found in the most popular psalm, which is Psalm 23. This is a psalm *for the living.* It is a mini-Bible, because in six short verses you will be led to receive God's blessings of salvation, overflow, and eternal life.

Each devotional message contains a central biblical theme, many Bible scriptures, and a message from God for you. Be ready to receive the blessings of salvation, overflow, and eternal life.

DR. RICKY BRANHAM is a television minister, interdenominational evangelist, senior pastor, and author who has traveled all over since the age of sixteen, spreading the good news of Jesus Christ. His television program, Ricky Branham Ministries, is on many networks in the United States and continues to grow nationally and internationally. Ricky and his wife, Victoria, have three children: Ricky, Riley, and Vera. For more information, please visit his website: www.rickybranham.com.

TRILOGY

ISBN 978-1-68556-891-7
90000
9 781685 568917

COMING SOON

Be on the lookout for more books in the *"Readings for Your Prayer Closet" Devotional Message Series* and other books and works by Dr. Ricky Branham.

CONTACTS, TELEVISION, AND SOCIAL MEDIA

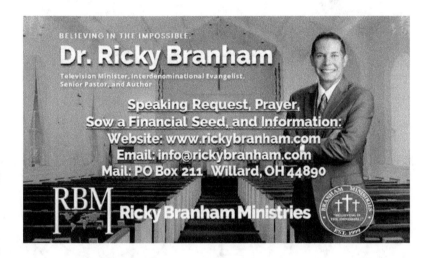

Ricky Branham Ministries

Printed in the USA
CPSIA information can be obtained
at www.ICGtesting.com
LVHW010301150624
783292LV00011B/403

9 798890 412621